D0982150

# THE
# KAMA SUTRA
# OF
# VATSYAYANA

# THE
# KAMA SUTRA
# OF
# VATSYAYANA

### THE CLASSIC HINDU TREATISE
### ON LOVE AND SOCIAL CONDUCT

**TRANSLATED BY SIR RICHARD F. BURTON**

*Foreword by Santha Rama Rau*

## INTRODUCTION BY JOHN W. SPELLMAN

**DORSET PRESS**
New York

This edition published by Dorset Press,
a division of Marboro Books Corporation,
by arrangement with E.P. Dutton.

1986 Dorset Press.

ISBN 0-88029-089-7

*Library of Congress Catalog Card Number:* 62-14720

Printed in the United States of America
M  19  18  17  16

# FOREWORD

One of the curious, but rather saddening, aspects of colonialism in Asia was that those of us who managed to get an education at all were largely educated in the language and culture of our foreign rulers. While we learned "A is for Apple" (in a part of the world where apples don't grow) and while we were lulled to sleep by parents (as I was) with long recitations from Shakespeare or Tennyson, we never had a chance to learn our own classics. It took a major effort and considerable intellectual stubbornness to explore, say, the great Sanskrit literature of ancient India.

At the same time, Westerners, more concerned with imposing foreign cultures on Asians than in learning about the cultures they were ruling, did not do a great deal toward fostering Asian studies in their own schools and colleges. For the most part, it has been only since the end of World War II, and the ensuing end of colonialism, that the great literature of Asia has been authoritatively translated and has found an audience in the West.

To me, in an age when we are urged by politicians to "understand" one another (although they never seem to tell us *how* to understand a foreign nation), the best bridge between cultures is literature. Most of us have not the opportunity to travel very widely, and even if we do, we usually cannot stay in a country long enough to "understand" or appreciate the culture. Writers—often accidentally—help us to this goal. They work from some core of truth in themselves and their perception of their world. In a way, this is a splendid and enjoyable short cut to that vital grasp of another civilization.

The *Kāma Sūtra* is a perfect case in point. Erotica, in the West, is considered rather wicked. Possibly it is the Puritan tradition that persuades people that sex is wrong —or, at least, something to be ashamed of and not to be mentioned in polite society. India, prudish as it is in many ways, seems on this score to be more realistic.

In most Hindu temples, in the many-layered carvings, you will usually see a panel depicting scenes from Hindu mythology or religious stories or various aspects of different deities. You will also see bas-reliefs of artists, musicians, dancers, in another panel. And, finally, you come to the erotic sculptures, boldly emblazoned in all their grandeur on the temple walls. In the very heart of a Śiva temple you will find the *liṅgam*—a classic phallic symbol of the god that is both the creator and destroyer. If it seems odd to foreigners that such a symbol should stand in a place of worship, to Indians it is the most natural, most obvious sign of "the Creator."

The point of these diverse subjects for sculpture is, of course, that Hindus feel that the full human life must concern itself with religious, sexual, and artistic experience. Consequently all must be shown in that center of Hindu life—the temple.

So, perhaps, if a reader comes to The *Kāma Sūtra* with modesty and an open mind, he will enjoy the literature and also learn an important facet of a foreign civilization.

SANTHA RAMA RAU

*New York City*

# CONTENTS

# INTRODUCTION

A literary and historical classic which has survived for over
a millennium should need no Introduction. The *Kāma
Sūtra,* however, is from India, and since much of the
Western world is still plunged in ignorance concerning
Indian civilization, an Introduction is not only justifiable,
it is necessary. Even today, schools give hardly more than
a casual passing reference to India, while colleges and uni-
versities, for the most part, still consider Indology an
esoteric subject. This is both shameful and harmful—
shameful in that academic institutions in a democratic society have failed in their responsibility to provide means
for enlightening its people about the major events and
ideas of the world's second largest country, and harmful
because in the absence of this knowledge serious errors in
interpretation and judgment have been made.

There is an Indian proverb which states that Truth is
like a diamond that has many facets and no view can
claim to see its entirety. *The Kāma Sūtra of Vātsyāyana* en-
ables us to see yet another view of society and customs.
This is well, for we cannot, without error and arrogance,
proclaim Truth merely by having recourse to our own history, values, and cultural foundations. The purpose of
studying about other countries is not to learn how we can
"deal" with them, but rather to learn what we can learn
from them. I am convinced that no one can justly claim
to interpret or understand contemporary Indian society,

thought, or problems without some knowledge of the major forces of ancient Indian civilization.

## THE BACKGROUND OF THE *Kāma Sūtra*

The object of this Introduction is to give some of the more important concepts, traditions, and legends relating to *kāma* in ancient India. This will help us to place the *Kāma Sūtra* within a framework which, we hope, shows both how it was affected by the society from which it arose and how, in turn, it affected aspects of Indian civilization. The *Kāma Sūtra* is not only a thoroughly delightful and readable book; it is also one of India's most important original works, giving us an insight into the history, politics, secular life, and social customs of ancient India. In view of the paucity of original sources at our disposal concerning ancient India, the evidence contained in the *Kāma Sūtra* becomes even more significant. In Sanskrit, *kāma* means desire, affection, love, lust, sensual pleasure, and the like. It is also one of the four *purusārthas* or goals of life. *Kāma* may also refer to the Indian god of love who, in some ways, is similar to Cupid or Eros in Western mythology. *Sūtra,* in this context, refers to the style of writing used by the author. This style consists of the use of aphorisms, short rules, or precepts. Thus, this work is called *Kāma Sūtra* owing to its subject and style.

There have been many other *Kāma Sūtra*s and this work by Vātsyāyana (pronounced as Vaht-syah'-yana) admits to being a compendium of previous texts written by authors lost in the haze of legend. Even the *Kāma Sūtra*s of those writers who seem to have some historical existence, such as Śvetāketu or Dattaka, are not available to us. The earliest writer, Nandin, is said to have composed his *Kāma Sūtra* in one thousand chapters. He is sometimes identified as the attendant of Śiva who recited the *Kāma Sūtra* while the high god was engaged in intercourse with his divine consort, Pārvatī. We cannot rule out the possibility that he actually lived, and the *Nandikeśvara* mentioned by Kokkola, another writer on *kāma,* may refer to Nandin. But there is no clear evidence of this and we really know nothing for certain about Nandin. Śvetāketu, the next author, is said to have abridged Nandin's work to five hundred chapters. He is mentioned in the *Chāndogya Upaniṣad* as Uddālaka's son who held discussions at an assembly house (*samiti*). The *Bṛhadāraṇyaka Upaniṣad* also speaks of Śvetāketu going to an assembly (*pariṣad*) of the Pañcāla tribes.[1] In a discussion which ensued, Śvetāketu had to admit ignorance concerning certain philosophical questions. The sexual symbolism of one of these is given in a later passage which says, "Woman is fire, O Gautama, her haunch the fuel; the hairs on her body the smoke; the *yoni,* the flame; intercourse, the coals; the fits of enjoyment, the sparks. The gods offer seed in this fire. From this offering man springs forth. He lives as long as he lives." [2]

Charms, magic, and incantations have a special place in the sphere of sex. This is true even today when manufacturers offer potions which are based on the principles of homeopathic or sympathetic magic to restore or increase virility. Like produces like, and the extract of some organ of an animal noted for its virility is supposed to produce virility in man. The dividing line between sex and religion is not always clear, and in all religions one is an

[1] *Bṛhadāraṇyaka Upaniṣad,* VI, 2:1. Passages such as these also indicate that the *pariṣad* and the *samiti* probably served similar functions both socially and politically.
[2] *Ibid.,* VI, 2:13.

aspect of the other. Another passage from the *Bṛhadāraṇ-yaka Upaniṣad* indicates this very well.

Prajāpāti (the Lord of Creation) thought to himself: "Let me provide a firm foundation." So he created woman. When he had created her, he honored her below. Therefore one should honor women below. He stretched out for himself that stone which projects.[3] With that he impregnated her. Her lap is a sacrificial altar; her hairs, the sacrificial grass; her skin, the soma-press. The two lips of the *yoni* are the fire in the middle. Verily, indeed, as great as is the world of the person who performs the *Vājapeya sacrifice* [the drink of strength], just as great is the world of him who practices sexual intercourse knowing this. He takes the good deeds of women to himself. But he who practices sexual intercourse without knowing this —women take his good deeds for themselves.[4]

It seems clear from the evidence that Śvetāketu dealt with the subject of *kāma*. His abridgment of Nandin's treatise was further summarized by Babhravya. All we know about the latter is that Vātsyāyana consulted his work of one hundred and fifty chapters.

Another writer was Dattācharya, the son of a Brahman of Mathura who settled in Pāṭaliputra (the modern Patna). His mother died shortly after his birth and he was adopted and given the name Dattaka (adopted son). Under the belief that prostitutes were skilled in worldly wisdom, he decided to obtain an education by keeping company with them. At their request he composed a treatise about their methods of operation and techniques. Except for the quotations from his work by Vātsyāyana in the *Kāma Sūtra* and a few references by various Indian

[3] The Śiva *liṅgam* widely worshiped throughout India today is invariably in the form of an elongated stone.
[4] *Bṛhadāraṇyaka Upaniṣad*, VI, 4:2-3.

dramatists, nothing remains. Other authors quoted by Vātsyāyana, such as Gonikaputra, Ghotakamukha, Gonarda, Charayana, and Suvarnanabha, also wrote on various aspects of the subject of *kāma*. We learn practically nothing about them from the available Sanskrit texts. Vātsyāyana appears to have consulted most of these works while writing his own *Kāma Sūtra,* which is divided into seven sections, thirty-six chapters, and sixty-four topics—a very considerable reduction of Nandin's one thousand chapters.

The date of Vātsyāyana is still a matter of some dispute. The dates assigned to him by scholars range from the sixth century B.C. to the sixth century A.D. The sixth-century B.C. dating can generally be discounted. It is largely based on a commentary, probably written in the thirteenth century A.D., from which the editor interpreted the numbers "twice twenty-four" as 2424 of the present Hindu time cycle, the *Kali yuga,* or 677–76 years before the Christian era. Available evidence seems to indicate that this date is either a forgery or a misinterpretation. This narrows the dating down from the fourth century B.C. to the sixth century A.D. Arguments exist for both extremes. There are many factors involved. Vātsyāyana mentions a number of kings in the course of his book. The inference is, of course, that these kings, such as Sātakarṇi Sātavāhana of Kuntal, and others, lived before Vātsyāyana. The Hāthigumpha inscription of about 150 B.C. mentions Sātakarṇi and suggests he was the third king of the Andhra dynasty. Unhappily, this reading is not clear and some scholars believe he was the thirteenth king of the dynasty. There is also the problem of the precise identification of Sātakarṇi.

Another method of dating compares the similarities of the *Kāma Sūtra* with the *Arthaśāstra* of Kauṭilya. The assumption is that Kauṭilya was the prime minister of

Candragupta Maurya whose dates are usually set at 322–298 B.C. While likenesses certainly exist between the two texts, the date of Kauṭilya is still disputed, and some scholars place him in the third century A.D. Vātsyāyana seems to be later than Kauṭilya and thus the fourth century A.D. is suggested for the *Kāma Sūtra*. The greatest of Sanskrit poets and dramatists, Kālidāsa,[5] regards Vātsyāyana as a venerable sage. Unfortunately, the date of Kālidāsa is itself subject to controversy, being placed anywhere between the first century B.C. and the fifth century A.D. Scholars continue to work on the problems of ancient Indian chronology and it is possible that one day we shall reach greater precision in our dating. The *Kāma Sūtra*, as a historical document, provides many clues which may help us to solve some of the chronological difficulties. At the present time, however, there is insufficient clear evidence to date the *Kāma Sūtra* accurately. In terms of Western history, it probably falls between the rule of Alexander and the reign of Constantine, i.e., the third century B.C. to the third century A.D. My own view is that it was written nearer the latter date.

Vātsyāyana's *Kāma Sūtra* is acknowledged to be one of the greatest Hindu books in existence. As a textbook on *kāma*, it is unequaled in the literature of any country. There are at least five commentaries on it excluding the *Vātsyāyana Sūtra Sāva* by Kṣemendra. Other famous Indian works on *kāma* include the *Rati-Rahasyam* by Kokkola, which may be placed about the twelfth century A.D. and which itself has at least four commentaries. The *Ananga Ranga*, probably the most famous text after the

[5] Perhaps his most famous work is *Śakuntalā*. The A. W. Ryder translation is available in paperback (D 40) from E. P. Dutton & Co., Inc.

*Kāma Sūtra,* was composed about the fifteenth century A.D. by Kalyāṇamalla. There are numerous minor Indian works on erotics as well.

There is a belief among many people that the Indians, and especially those of ancient times, spent their lives wrapped in meditation about future lives and spiritual problems. Some even suggest that this "other-worldly" aspect of Indian life was responsible for the political disunity, lack of industrialization, and general apathy toward life which they felt was an inherent part of Indian civilization. India, for many even today, is a symbol for mysticism, yoga, and snake charmers. The other stereotype is to regard her as a backward land of teeming millions where the poverty-stricken people raise their bony hands for a crust of bread. Both of these beliefs are the result of colossal ignorance.

### THE PURUṢĀRTHAS

What are the goals of life? What are the objects of human existence? Many of us do not have an answer to such questions. We fumble for solutions and perhaps suggest that man's aim is to continue the species, enjoy himself, serve God, or something else. Western philosophy has been reluctant to give us a categorical and definitive answer. In India this was not so. From very ancient times the goals of human life (*puruṣārthas*) were defined and established. They were listed as *dharma, artha, kāma,* and *mokṣa.* The first three, known as the *trivarga,* are to be practiced in this life, and if done successfully will lead to *mokṣa,* which constitutes the ultimate liberation of the soul or spirit (*ātman*) from the cycle of rebirths (*saṃsāra*) through which man must pass in order to purify himself from all evil before merging into the cosmic soul (*Brahman*). This is a simplified explanation (and therefore subject to the errors which all generalizations must contain) of the concept of *mokṣa* on which literally thousands of volumes have been written. Although one may achieve *mokṣa* by following the paths of knowledge, faith, good works, or devotion, it is a goal which is achieved through the successful fulfillment of other goals and not as an isolated or independent object.

Of the threefold objects, *dharma* is generally acknowledged to be the most important. *Dharma* means right conduct, in accordance with what is proper, cosmic law, the natural order of things, righteousness, and the like. It has kinship with the Western concept of natural law and the Chinese idea of *tao*. It is undoubtedly one of the most important concepts in Indian thought. "There is nothing higher than Dharma. Even a weak person is certain of defeating a more powerful one by Dharma, as a house-holder by the king. Thus, Dharma is Truth. Therefore they say of a person who speaks the Truth (*Satya*), he speaks Dharma or of a person who speaks Dharma, he speaks the Truth. They are both the same." [6] To act *adharma,* or against Dharma, must indeed be contrary to the objects of life. *Dharma* is said by some texts to be the source of *artha* and *kāma.* Even the *Kāma Sūtra* recognizes this and states that *dharma* is more important than its own subject matter. The great Hindu lawgiver, Manu, says that although one should strive for all goals, if there is a conflict with *dharma,* then *artha* or *kāma* should be given up. The injunctions of the ancient texts are clear on the point that life must be lived in accordance with *dharma.* There is a

[6] *Bṛhadāraṇyaka Upaniṣad,* I, 4:14. The motto of the Republic of India is *Satyam eva jayati*—Truth always conquers.

pattern, an order, a "rightness" for all things. In nature, it may be more obvious than in human society. Nevertheless, it is everywhere, and man should guide his personal and public affairs in accordance with it.

*Artha* means the accumulation of material goods, the pursuit of economic interests, obtaining wealth and material security, and other such ideals. Certainly other cultures have endorsed this view, but I do not think that they have expressly stated it as one of the objects of life. Not *the* object, mark you, but only one of them, even though a very important one. Those who visualize the Indians as "other-worldly" seem to ignore this thought basic to Hinduism. The concept of Indian society makes two special provisions for the promotion of *artha*. As a class,[7] the Vaiśyas have as their special duty trading and other mercantile interests. The householder or *Gṛhastha*, as one of the four ideal stages of life,[8] should accumulate economic possessions and provide for the security of his family. Thus, *artha* pervades both the social organization and the individual within the framework of Hinduism. As one might expect, Kauṭilya, the author of the *Arthaśāstra*, says that *artha* is the highest of the three since *dhàrma* and *kāma* arise from *artha*. This, however, is a minority opinion and most authorities have no hesitation in proclaiming *dharma* as supreme.

The third *trivarga* is *kāma*. The *Dharmaśāstra*s and

[7] There are four classes in Hindu society: the Brahmans or priestly class; the Kṣatriyas, who are the warriors and political rulers; the Vaiśyas or mercantile class; and the Śūdras, whose duty is to serve the other three. Within each of these classes are numerous castes.

[8] The four ideal stages of life are: (1) the *Brahmacārin* or student stage; (2) the *Gṛhastha* or householder who raises and provides for a family; (3) the *Vānaprastha* who retires to the forest toward a more spiritual life; and (4) the *Sannyāsin* or wandering ascetic seeking *mokṣa*.

most other texts rank it as the least important of all. This does not mean that it is of minor significance. All of the *trivarga*s are extremely important and, ideally, one has an obligation to all three. It is only when there is a conflict that distinctions need be made as to priority. Even the *Kāma Sūtra* is explicit about this and points out that there are exceptions, such as *artha* being the most important for a king and *kāma* for a public woman. The importance of *kāma* is stressed by Bhima as a reply to Yudhisthira's question as to which of the three should be foremost.

One without Kāma never wishes for Artha. One without Kāma never wishes for Dharma. One who is destitute of Kāma can never feel and wish. For this reason, Kāma is the foremost of the three. . . . Everything is pervaded by the principle of Kāma. A man outside the pale of Kāma never is, was or will be seen in this world. As butter represents the essence of curds, even so is Kāma the essence of Artha and Dharma. Oil is better than oil seeds. Ghee is better than sour milk. Flowers and fruits are better than wood. Just so, Kāma is better than Dharma and Artha. As nectar is extracted from flowers, so is Kāma to be extracted from these two. Kāma is the parent of Dharma and Artha. Kāma is the soul of these two." [9]

Similar ideas are also found in a number of other ancient Indian texts.

[9] *Mahābhārata,* Śānti Parvan, 167. The *Mahābhārata* is the greatest book of India and leads to more understanding of that country than any other single work. Unhappily, most Westerners are either ignorant of it or frightened of its length. There are some unsatisfactory abridgments of it, but they are no substitute for the full work which may be available in some of the larger libraries. To read an abridgment is to try to visualize the ocean by looking at a glass of water. The P. C. Roy English edition is easily obtainable from Indian booksellers or directly from the publishers: Oriental Publishing Co., 11/D Arpuli Lane, Calcutta 12.

Sexual desire is an obvious innate urge of all creatures, including mankind. There is no point in attempting to ignore this; indeed, that would be harmful. Sexual pleasures are also one of the most delightful joys of which man partakes. That they should become a dull routine chore merely for the purpose of reproduction is not only a tragedy in a very real sense; it is a gross denial of what we are. The *Kāma Sūtra* pleads for a balance of these values. Liquor in moderation is pleasant; intoxication is repulsive. Just so, excessive sexual indulgence and promiscuity are *adharma*. The *Kāma Sūtra* clearly condemns the latter. But it also insists that sexual knowledge broadens the horizons for man's rightful claim to sexual pleasures.

The idea of romantic love is sometimes considered to be a Western phenomenon and it is even suggested that such an idea does not exist at all in India. Much of this thinking is based on the understanding that love is not a prime factor for Hindus before they get married. To a large extent this is true. As a Hindu would say, "Once the kettle is boiling, the water can only become cooler." Marriage is understood as the entrance to love and not an anticlimax to it. Nevertheless, the idea of a love-marriage has been recognized in India from ancient times and the lawbooks give it legal status as one of the various kinds of marriage, even if they do not wholly approve of it. The *Mahābhārata* and other Indian sources contain numerous stories in which romantic love plays a very great part. We shall look at some of these legends later.

KĀMA—THE GOD

Hinduism personifies a number of abstract qualities. Gods become the embodiment of a particular quality, such as the Vedic god Varuṇa being the lord of Dharma and water. Justice or punishment (*daṇḍa*) is also anthropomorphized as the god Daṇḍa. Kāma, the Indian god of love and sexual desire, shoots his flower arrows from a bow made of sugar cane strung with a row of bees. Like Eros, this youthful Indian god of love shoots his flowery arrows without regard to caste, customs, or public opinion. No one, whether mortal or god, has ever been able to ignore the shafts of Kāma or, as he is sometimes known, Ananga (the Body-less One). Even the great god Śiva was not entirely immune from him, and the following story tells of their conflict and why Kāma is also known as Ananga.

Satī was the daughter of Dakśa Prajāpati and the first consort of Śiva. She was driven to grief and finally to death because her father continually insulted and abused her divine lord. Śiva went to a lonely corner of the Himālaya mountains and wrapped himself in meditation. The demon Tāraka was at that time harassing the gods, who were powerless against him. Indeed, it had been prophesied that only the son of Śiva and a daughter of the Himālayas could be successful in defeating Tāraka. Satī had taken rebirth as Pārvatī, the beautiful daughter of the Mountain, but Śiva continued in meditation. The gods resolved to marry Śiva again to Pārvatī, who, in any case, refused to have any other husband. She went to the great god to make offerings, but he completely ignored her. Meanwhile, Indra, the king of the gods, had secured the services of Kāma in this venture. When the god of love released his flower shaft at Śiva, even he could not remain oblivious to it. The disturbed Mahā Yogi (Great Ascetic) looked around in anger for the source of his discomfort and, seeing Kāma, at once burned him to ashes with fire that issued from his third eye. The beautiful Pārvatī resigned herself to asceticism near her lord. He finally noticed and fell in love with her. At a great ceremony they were married and she gave birth to the war-god Skanda. It was he who, in fulfillment of the prophecy, killed Tāraka.

Rati (Pleasure), the wife of Kāma, was filled with grief at the death of her husband and blamed Indra for sending her consort on this dangerous mission. Indra promised that her husband would return to her as Pradyumna, the grandson of Kṛṣṇa. Rati then disguised herself under the name of Mayavati and began to live in the house of a demon king called Sambara. According to prophecy, Pradyumna killed the demon Sambara and married Mayavati. Another version has it that Pradyumna is the son of Kṛṣṇa by his first queen Rukmini. Rukma, Rukmini's brother, has a daughter (presumably Rati in another birth) who marries Pradyumna. In spite of their kinship through marriage, Rukma vows vengeance on Kṛṣṇa and is finally killed by Balarāma, Kṛṣṇa's brother. Pradyumna's son, Aniruddha, falls in love with Uṣa, the daughter of a demon, and after a battle in which Krsna defeats Uṣa's father, Vanāsura, the two lovers are married. So much for a partial genealogy of Kāma.

### EMBLEMS OF KĀMA

Kāma has as his attendants a troop of apsarases (divine nymphs), one of whom carries his standard which bears a sea monster or fish. This is significant in view of the fact that the ornaments of Kāma are the conch shell and the lotus.[10] The kinship of all these elements with water, a symbol of creativity, is immediately obvious. The lotus is certainly the most remarkable symbol of India. It has per-

[10] *Viṣṇu Purāṇa*, III, 73:20.

vaded practically every aspect of Indian culture. Unfortunately, there has been very little research on this subject by scholars. The most sacred and powerful *mantra* (sacred formulae) of Tantric Buddhism is translated as, "The Jewel is indeed within the Lotus." This auspicious charm is interpreted as meaning that the principle of creativity finds expression through the semen (jewel) in the womb (lotus). There is, of course, more meaning than merely this simple statement, but it is clear that the lotus is undoubtedly a symbol (among other things) of the female sex organ (*yoni*). It was from the cosmic lotus that this world, including the gods, was created,[11] and future worlds will have the same origin. Invariably, female beauty (and sometimes male as well) is described in Indian literature by analogy with the lotus. The other ornament of Kāma is the conch shell, which also comes from water and, like the lotus, resembles the *yoni*.[12] It is associated with female fertility and regarded as a very auspicious object. In Hindu iconography it is intimately connected with the god Viṣṇu. In ancient Greece, pearls and sea shells were likewise associated with marriage and fertility.[13] The emblems of Kāma are therefore by no means haphazard or unsuitable.

Springtime has been dedicated to love and sexual activity in popular and religious lore all over the world. It is the season of rejuvenation. The birds and the bees (a phrase frequently used as a sexual expression) appear

[11] Another version, significantly enough, makes the source of creation a golden egg.

[12] While *yoni* has the primary meaning of the female sex organ and is used throughout the *Kāma Sūtra* in that sense, it is worth noting that "water" or "place of origin" is a secondary meaning.

[13] There seems to be a clear relationship between the popular myth that eating oysters increases sexual potency and the custom of giving a pearl as an engagement ring with what we have cited above.

after the long winter season, and the flowers of spring, whether propelled by Kāma or not, have an excitement all their own. The spring wind is also, according to Indian literature, a powerful ally of Kāma. It is not only in the spring of the year but also in the spring of our lives that Kāma gives us most attention. Unhappy indeed is he who does not profit from it.

King Yayāti was denied that period of life and cursed by Śukra to grow old at once. The curse of a god or a Ṛṣi must always be fulfilled. There is no power capable of completely rescinding such a curse once it has been made. It can only be modified, and in King Yayāti's case, he was allowed to retain his youth only if he could get one of his five sons to agree to accept the curse in his stead. His eldest son, who was heir to the throne, saw no joy in growing old before his time and refused the request of his father. One after another, his sons turned him down until King Yayāti went to his youngest son, Pūru. He begged him to accept the curse of old age for a thousand years so that the king could have his youth for the same period of time. Pūru was moved by his father's plight and with filial devotion exchanged his youth for the king's old age and infirmities. For a thousand years Yayāti delighted himself with his beautiful wife, Śarmiṣṭha. At the end of that time, he took back his old age and returned youth, as well as the throne, to his youngest son.[14] Yayāti had enjoyed *kāma* for a thousand years, but even he was forced to admit that *kāma* can never quench *kāma;* on the contrary, love-making stimulates desire.

---

[14] There are a number of versions of the legend of Yayāti, just as there are of the legend of Devāpi where the youngest son also received the throne in violation of the rule of primogeniture which operated in ancient India.

## THE HOLI FESTIVAL

We have already seen that Kāma was reduced to ashes by Śiva when he disturbed the austerities of the high god by trying to inflame the latter with love for Pārvatī. There are variations in most legends of Indian literature and this one is no exception. Another tradition says that when Śiva burnt Kāma, the followers of Śiva began to shout abuses at him and demanded the restoration of the god of love. Śiva agreed but ordered that his punishment of Kāma should be commemorated by the annual burning of the latter's image. Whoever obeyed this injunction should be rewarded by banishing those evils which confronted them.[15] This ceremony of burning an effigy of Kāma is carried out during the month of Phālguna at the approach of the spring season, especially during the three or four days preceding the full moon. As with the Christian spring rite of Easter, the date of the Hindu festival of Holi changes each year. This ancient ceremony is still carried out in India today, although in most places its original significance has been lost. Indeed, it is more than likely that the interpretation that we have given of this festival is merely a justification of a spring rite which existed in times of remote antiquity. In the same way, although the Easter festival has marked Christian overtones, it is nevertheless an extension of the Babylonian fertility rite in which the goddess Ishtar was reunited with her lover Tammuz.

The method of celebrating the Holi festival varies widely in India today. It is a time of considerable merry-making, although few women take part in the more bois-

[15] Another account suggests that the purpose of the Holi festival is to frighten away the demoness Dhundhi, who inflicts various diseases upon children.

terous activities. The streets and bazaars are filled with people throwing colored powders or squirting colored water on each other. As with the arrows of Kāma, caste distinctions are forgotten for a while and everyone mixes freely in the crowds. People go around daubing red powder [16] on each other's forehead and embracing. Holi is probably the most popular festival in India today. It is a great deal of fun and good will seems to pervade the atmosphere. One Hindu, while smearing colored powder across my face, told me that this was the day on which all grudges and ill will were forgotten.

If the popular gaiety lacks some (but by no means all) of the more explicit religious aspects of the Holi festival, this does not mean that they have been totally forgotten in India. The squirting of water may have several meanings. It may be a symbol of the creative principle, a method of purification, or to be used in conjunction with the fire that burns Kāma. The embracing and lack of caste distinctions have an obvious association with the god of love. In the villages, however, some customs differ, and as Indian village life has always preserved traditional values, it is to the local ceremonies that we must look for a clearer view of the associations between the Holi festival and Kāma.

It is in some of the village ceremonies especially that we can observe the relationship of Kāma to fire (*agni*). This is significant in a number of ways. The passion of love is often compared with the heat of fire. It was by fire that Śiva reduced Kāma to ashes. Moreover, in Indian

---

[16] Professor A. L. Basham, in his excellent book, *The Wonder That Was India* (London: Sidgwick and Jackson, 1954), is probably correct when he suggests (p. 207) that the red powder is a survival of a bloody fertility ceremony. There is much evidence to support this view. Basham's book is undoubtedly the best available for anyone wishing a readable comprehensive survey of ancient Indian civilization.

literature, Agni, the god of fire, is often identified with
Kāma, the god of love. They are both penetrating, devour-
ing, and even purifying elements. The color red which
predominates during Holi also symbolizes both fire and
love. The fact that Holi is known as the great fire festival
of Western India is not without significance.

Abbott describes one of these ceremonies:

Three months before Holi a site is chosen for the burning of
Kāma's image, and is cleansed and sprinkled with water.
Then every Sunday until Holi a party of men go out for
Shikar (a big game hunt), the first expedition with this ob-
ject being made on the day following the Sankranaṇa called
Kari. On their way to the jungle the men worship an Ari tree
(*Bauhinia racemosa*) and place near it their guns, their instruments and even their sticks and scythes, and worship them.
When the first animal is shot this victim and the successful
hunter are worshipped in the jungle; a procession is formed,
women wave Ārtī round the victim of the chase and the
hunters, and the slain animals are all placed on the site where
Kāma's image is to be burned later. The blood of the slain
animals is collected in a tin, and a small spot of blood is
daubed on the doors of all the leading men in the village, and
a communal feast is made from the flesh of the victims.[17]

The night before Holi, people in the village visit each
other's houses and collect old clothes to be burned on the
headless image of Kāma. On Holi morning, a coconut is
painted like a head and attached to the body of Kāma.
With a good deal of gaiety the villagers steal wood, cow
dung, and other fuel for the fire. Obscene words are written freely on the clothes of the participants. Kāma's pyre
is built up, and either on Holi or the following day (Pra-

[17] J. Abbott, *The Keys of Power—A Study of Indian Ritual and
Belief* (London: Methuen & Co., Inc., 1932), p. 198.

tipadā), the image is burned. The ashes are collected and distributed around the village as a protection against evil. Red water is sprinkled by the villagers on each other, and there is much singing, dancing, and general rowdiness in which the prostitutes participate.[18] Characteristics of other ceremonies are the erection of a pole bearing symbols of fertility either in the center of Kāma's fire or nearby, sprinkling the ashes from the pyre with seed or scattering it on the granary floor, and other factors which suggest a strong influence for fertility. The time for burning the image of Kāma varies, but noon is the most usual.

The Holi festival, then, is the Indian spring fertility festival. Kāma is the obvious god to be associated with these rites. His role as a god, however, is decreasing in India today, and this partially accounts for the confusing of traditions and legends. Nevertheless, it remains as one of the most important days in the Hindu calendar, and its obvious associations with the subject matter of the *Kāma Sūtra* dictates its mention here.

### LOVE AMONG THE GODS

The dividing line between men and gods has never been very clear in India. If the gods are gods, then the Brahmans are also declared to be gods by certain texts. In ancient India, at least, divinity was freely and easily acquired. Not only individuals, but trees, rivers, stones, and cows were, amongst others, invested with sanctity. Natural forces were also personified as gods. Therefore, in discussing love among the gods, we must appreciate that the implications of the term "gods" in India is far more extensive than in Greek or other Western religious beliefs,

[18] *Ibid.*, p. 198-99.

even though we shall find parallels, in this area, between the ancient Greek and Roman gods and those of India.

Incest among the gods produces a certain amount of theological embarrassment. Why gods should commit incest is a provocative question, but beyond the purview of this essay. The legend of Brahmā and his daughter is given in a number of ancient Hindu texts and is well worth our attention.[19] As usual, there are variations, but the *Matsya Purāṇa* relates most of the important points.

This story is told by Viṣṇu in his incarnation (*avatāra*) as a fish (*mātsya*),[20] when Manu asked him how Lord Brahmā created the universe and why he has four heads. Viṣṇu replied that after Brahmā had practiced austerities and revealed sacred knowledge, he then created through his will or desire the ten sages. He then produced Dharma from his breast, Kāma from his heart, Anger from his brows, Greed from his lips, Delusion from his intellect, Arrogance from his egotism, Delight from his throat, Death from his eyes, and the Ṛṣi Bhārata from his hands. After Lord Brahmā had created all these, he was still not

[19] References to this matter are found in *Aitareya Brāhmaṇa*, III, 33; *Śatapatha Brāhmaṇa*, I, 7:4:1ff., XIV, 4:2:1ff.; *Mātsya Purāṇa*, III, 32ff.; *Bhāgavata Purāṇa*, III, 12:28ff.

[20] There are nine incarnations of the high god Viṣṇu. The tenth is to come. The nine *avatāras* are briefly given as follows: (1) *Mātsya* or the fish, when Viṣṇu came to save Manu from the universal flood. Manu was warned and told to build a boat and to bring seven Ṛṣis or sages and the seeds of all things. The fish bore the ship until the flood had passed. (2) *Kūrma* or the tortoise, in which Viṣṇu descended to the bottom of the sea of the world to recover articles lost in the deluge and produced the fourteen precious things. (3) *Varāha* or the boar, when Viṣṇu saved the world from a demon who had carried it to the depths of the sea. He killed the demon and raised the world on his tusk. (4) *Nara-siṃha* or the man-lion, who appeared in that form to foil a boon that the gods had granted to a wicked king that he should not be killed either by gods or man or animals.

satisfied and wanted someone to relieve him of the task of creation. He began to call on the goddess Gāyatri, also known as Sāvitrī, Sarasvatī, Brahmāṇi, and other names. She appeared in the form of a girl from the female side of Brahmā's body, and was taken as his daughter. Her beauty was astonishing, and the creator, smitten by the arrows of Kāma, gazed upon her, repeatedly saying, "What a beautiful figure! What a beautiful figure!" At these remarks, the sons of Brahmā, led by the sage Vasiṣṭha, were filled with indignation and disgust at their father's attitude toward their sister. But Brahmā was so much absorbed that he did nothing but continue to gaze at Sāvitrī repeating, "What a beautiful figure!" Sāvitrī then began to walk around Brahmā, but his sense of shame would not allow him to turn his face. In order to look at her, he created four heads on himself so that he could see her in whatever direction she went. Sāvitrī then went to heaven, and as she did, Brahmā created a fifth face on the top of his head, which he afterward covered with his matted locks. Through such usage, the High God lost his powers gained through asceticism and asked his sons to carry on

---

(5) *Vāmana* or the dwarf, who appeared to declaim the three worlds of gods, men, and demons. The dwarf asked for three paces of land and as Viṣṇu obtained the worlds of gods and men in two paces he left the lower one in the demon's possession. (6) As *Paraśu-Rāma*, or Rāma with the ax, he cleared the world of Kṣatriyas who were trying to establish themselves over the Brahmans. (7) As *Rāma* he destroyed the demon king Rāvaṇa. These exploits are narrated in the Hindu epic *The Rāmāyana*. (8) As *Kṛṣṇa* he destroyed the tyrant king Kansa. (9) The *Buddha* incarnation suggests that in this form Viṣṇu deceived demons and wicked men by causing their destruction since they refused to accept the authority of the Veda, the gods, and neglected caste duties. In reality, this *avatāra* represents a compromise between the Brahmans and the Buddhists. (10) *Kalki* will appear seated on a white horse to destroy this evil age in which we now live and to establish righteousness.

with the work of creation. Brahmā followed Sāvitrī, married her, and they lived together in a lotus for one hundred years. The Purāṇa then points out that no question arises regarding prohibited acts of the gods since they do not reap the fruits of their *karma* (actions) as do mortals.[21] A further justification of Brahmā's action is given by noting that Brahmā is the lord of the Vedas and Sāvitrī is the goddess of the Vedas. They are therefore inseparable, and to unite the Vedas with the sacred prayer can surely be no evil.

Nevertheless, Brahmā was filled with shame at not having concealed his passion before his sons. He became angry at Kāma and cursed him saying, "The reasons for which you fired your arrows at me will cause you, before long, to be reduced to ashes by Śiva when you act the same way toward him." Kāma remonstrated against this curse and argued that Brahmā himself had created him to kindle the passion of love in men and women and that he had only carried out his maker's mandate, which had not excluded Brahmā from being subject to his arrows. After hearing Kāma's entreaties, Brahmā allowed that the god of love should be reborn first in the family of king Yadu and then as the son of Kṛṣṇa, and after having enjoyed himself, Kāma would be reborn as the son of Vatsa in the family of king Bhārata. From that time, he would live until the dissolution that closes the reign of Vidyadharas (a type of demigod) and then return to Brahmā.

From Varuṇa, the lord of morality and waters, we should expect conduct befitting his position. Yet even he,

[21] This must be considered a minority view since most texts indicate quite clearly that through *karma* gods may become men and vice versa. Further, gods do reap the fruits of their *karma* (action, cause, destiny, etc.) as Kāma (the god of love) does in these cases.

under the influence of Kāma, committed an act of *adharma*. Bhadrā, the daughter of Soma, was unrivaled for her beauty, and the Ṛṣi, Utathya, had been selected as her husband. After the marriage took place, Varuṇa went to the woods where Utathya lived, abducted Bhadrā, and took her to his palatial mansion surrounded by six hundred thousand beautiful lakes, and encompassing all objects of enjoyment. In that palace the Lord of the Waters made love to Bhadrā. When Utathya learned from the sage Nārada that Varuṇa had ravished his wife, he told Nārada angrily to demand her return. Varuṇa refused to obey and threw Nārada out of his house by his neck. When this news reached Utathya his anger knew no bounds, and through his spiritual power he caused all the waters to dry up. Although this made the Lord of the Waters very unhappy and dismal, he still refused to give up Utathya's wife. Utathya then commanded the Earth to show land where the six hundred thousand lakes existed and at once sterile ground appeared in their place. To the Sarasvatī River, Utathya made the request that she dry up and that the area through which she traveled be no longer regarded as sacred ground.[22] When that region in which Lord Varuṇa lived became dry, he went back to Utathya with Bhadrā and returned her to her rightful lord. The Ṛṣi rejoiced and set the world and Varuṇa free from the distress he had inflicted through his spiritual energy.[23]

Gods seem rather to like earthly women, and one of their favorite tricks is to seduce these beautiful earthlings, disguised as their husbands. Zeus was very fond of this game and his exploits are a well-known feature of Greek

[22] Even today in India, the Sarasvatī River is a dried-up stream.
[23] This legend is told in the Anuśāsana Parvan of the *Mahābhārata*, 154:10*ff.*

mythology. Indra, the king of the gods in early Hinduism, had a similar penchant. Neither his haggard but faithful wife, Indrāṇī, nor his host of heavenly apsarases (sensuous divine damsels) could keep him from these diversions. This divine profligate could appear anywhere and assume the disguise most likely to cause beautiful damsels to surrender their charms to him. This is not to say that all the women were duped by this libertine. Ahalyā clearly recognizes the king of the gods with all his trappings and finds him a rather refreshing change from her husband. She welcomes and indeed encourages her lover to continue these escapades with her.[24] Indra clearly did not set a very good example for mankind to follow, and, as a result, we are told this practice of seducing other men's wives has come into this world. Indeed it has. Medieval European literature, especially Boccaccio's *Decameron,* suggests that men were not above assuming the disguise of gods to obtain the same favors for which gods assumed the disguise of men.

These selected stories from Indian literature obviously do not reflect the general tenor of Hindu works, and even in those we have cited there is often a moralistic damnation reserved for the seducer. It is an uneven battle to fight against Kāma, and perhaps we cannot blame too much those who lose. Let me relate to you another story about Kāma—a rather delightful one, I think. Certainly the text claims it is meritorious to hear. It comes from the Vana Parvan of that great Indian treasury, the *Mahābhārata.*[25]

[24] Indra was not very overjoyed when he found that Nahuṣa, a temporary king of the gods, was enjoying the charms of his own wife, Indrāṇī. With righteous indignation he killed the violator of his marriage bed. Are men, then, not like gods? For a fuller account of this story see the *Rāmāyaṇa,* I, 48.

[25] *Mahābhārata,* Vana Parvan, Sections 45-46.

Arjuna, one of the five sons of Pāṇḍu and the person to whom Kṛṣṇa addresses himself in the *Bhāgavad Gītā* portion of the *Mahābhārata,* is invited by Indra, king of the gods, to visit his celestial palace. Arjuna lived for five years in the palace of Indra, during which time he learned a great deal and also received certain celestial weapons to use against his adversaries and the forces of evil. Indra observes that during his visit Arjuna continually glances at the beautiful heavenly apsaras, Urvaśī. Indra is delighted by this turn of events and says that just as Arjuna has, through him, learned all about weapons and other arts, he should now learn how to behave in the company of women. He therefore instructs his messenger to request Urvaśī to visit Arjuna for this purpose. The messenger describes the virtues and beauty of Arjuna to the apsaras while Kāma shoots a few of his flowery arrows. Urvaśī needs very little coaxing and prepares for a visit to Arjuna that very evening. Let us follow (at a respectful distance) as she makes her way toward Arjuna's mansion.

And having taken a bath she adorned herself in charming ornaments and splendid garlands of celestial fragrance. And inflamed by the god of love, and her heart pierced through and through by the shafts shot by Kāma, keeping in view the beauty of Arjuna, she mentally sported with him on a wide and excellent bed laid over with celestial sheets. And when the twilight had deepened and the moon had risen, that apsaras of broad hips went forth to seek the house of Arjuna. And in that atmosphere with her long curly hair in which was woven many jasmine flowers, she looked extremely beautiful. With her beauty and grace and the charm of the movements of her eyebrows and of her soft voice and her face radiant as the moon, she seemed to challenge the moon himself as she glided along. And as she went, her deep, finely tapering, black-nippled breasts, adorned with a golden necklace, and rubbed with the fragrant salve of sandalwood, trembled up and down. And as a result of the weight of her breasts she was forced to bend slightly at every step, creating three folds in her beautiful waist. And her thighs of faultless shape, the place of the temple of the god of love swelling like a hill, furnished with fair and high and round hips, graced with golden lace, wrapped in sheer garments and capable of shaking the sainthood of Ṛṣis, appeared extremely lovely. Her feet, in which the ankles were shallow and possessing long copper-colored toes arched like a turtle's back, glittered, being ornamented with rows of little bells. And exhilarated by a little liquor which she had taken and excited by desire and by her various sweet wiles and expressing a sensation of delight, she looked more beautiful than ever. And although heaven was filled with wonders, yet when Urvaśī went in such a way, the Siddhas, Cāraṇas, and Gandharvas regarded her as the loveliest wonder upon which they had cast their eyes. With the upper part of her body draped in a garment of fine texture which shimmered with the colors of the clouds, she looked like a sickle of the moon in the sky as it glides along wrapped in clouds. And with the speed of the winds or of the mind thus did the brightly smiling one reach the house of Arjuna, son of Pāṇḍu. When she had come to the gate there, Urvaśī of beautiful eyes was announced by the gatekeeper to Arjuna. And (having received permission) she entered that delightful and excellent palace. With a mind filled with anxious doubts, he came to meet her in the night. And as soon as the son of Pṛthā saw Urvaśī he lowered his eyes from modesty and in greeting her, he showed the apsaras that respect which is offered to a person of superior station. Arjuna spoke, "O thou foremost of the apsarases, I bow my head before thee in greeting. I wait upon thee as thy servant."

At these words, Urvaśī was completely taken aback and told Arjuna all that had passed between the messenger and herself. Not only had Indra sent her, but she, herself, struck by the arrows of Kāma, was filled with desire for him. Arjuna protested, claiming that if he had gazed upon her, it was as a mother—a feeling of respect for one's superiors. Urvaśī countered by saying that the apsarases were free to love whom they would and that no loss of merit was incurred by making love to them. Arjuna insisted that she was the parent of his race and an object of reverence and honor to him. Urvaśī was filled with rage and frustration. She had been repulsed and her desire had not been quenched. She turned in anger to Arjuna and cursed him saying, "Since you refuse a woman who has come to you at the command of your father and of her own free will, a woman, besides, who is pierced by the shafts of Kāma, therefore you shall pass your time in the company of women, destitute of manhood and scorned as a eunuch." Still trembling with rage, Urvaśī turned and went back to her own house. Arjuna was rather taken aback by this treatment and repeated the tale to his friends, and finally it reached Indra. He said that the curse would work to Arjuna's benefit, since in the thirteenth year of exile from the kingdom of Pāṇḍu, he would disguise himself as a dancer and a eunuch would have no difficulty in obtaining access to the female apartments of the palace to give instruction. "The desires of the man that listens to this story of the son of Pāṇḍu never run after lustful ends. The foremost of men, by listening to this account of the extremely pure conduct of Arjuna, the son of the lord of the celestials, becomes empty of pride, arrogance, wrath, and other faults and, ascending to heaven, enjoys his delights in bliss." [26]

[26] The moral which J. J. Meyer, *Sexual Life in Ancient India* (London: Routledge and Kegan Paul, 1930), p. 328, gives is, "If a foolish man will not when a foolish woman will, then he has to pay for it heavily."

There are many other stories of love among the gods or between other notables in Indian literature. The delightful legends of King Saṃvarṇa and Tapatī, Nala and Damayantī, Śakuntalā, Kṛṣṇa and Rādhā are only a few among many. There can be no doubt from these stories that the idea of romantic love was well known in India. The joy and delights that spring from Kāma are a well-known theme in ancient Indian literature. But Kāma is also the source of suffering. The slightest touch of love is compared to a fire in the hollow of a tree which burns roots, trunk, and all, leaving only a useless shell as a mockery. If spring is an ally of the god of love, so is Mṛtyu, the goddess of death. That despair in love sometimes leads to a longing for death or death itself is well known. Are there any sorrows greater than those of love? Perhaps love is the only sorrow and all grief stems from love. How great was the grief of Rāma when he knew that his beloved Sītā had been abducted from their forest cottage! [27] At first he thinks her absence is a joke she is playing upon him. But it rapidly becomes obvious that this is not so. He goes hysterical and runs with tears in his eyes, asking every animal and tree to tell him of the whereabouts of his beloved. There are no answers and the distraught Rāma wanders to a lake filled with beautiful lotuses and fishes. This calms him for a while and he speaks to his brother Lakṣmaṇa:

Look, Lakṣmaṇa, Lake Pampā is crystal clear like the jewel in a cat's eye, with its wealth of lotuses that blossom by day. See the lovely woods which fringe its banks rising as though to

---

[27] The *Rāmāyana* is the second great epic of India and very much shorter than the *Mahābhārata*. The abduction of Sītā by the demon Rāvaṇa and Rāma's exploits in recapturing the woman who even today is regarded as the model ideal wife by Hindus occupies a central portion of this epic. The three volumes may be obtained from the Oriental Publishing Co., 11/D Arpuli Lane, Calcutta 12.

the height of mountains. The branches of these trees look like the peaks of a hill. Even I who am dried up with sorrow at the loss of Sītā and stricken with grief at the thought of Bharata's sufferings find something to make my heart glad at this sight. See how the deep green grass strewn with blossoms of many colors appears like a beautiful checkered blanket spread on the ground. The flower-crowned creepers clasp in embrace the branches of the blossom laden trees. This is spring! This is the season of love! Feel how gently the breeze is blowing. See the flowers in full blossom and smell their fragrance which permeates the forest. The breeze blows the trees and their flowers drop like rain from the clouds. The wind seems to be dancing with the flowers; some have dropped to the ground, others are still falling, and yet others are clasping to the trees. . . . the trees are embracing one another by having their branches interlaced by the breezes and the perfume of wild honey has intoxicated the humming bees. The hills with the blossoming trees on their crests seem to have a crown of jewels on their heads. O son of Sumitrā [Lakṣmaṇa] since I am without Sītā, this spring only brings me sorrow and the ruthless pangs of love pierce me. Listen! It is as if the sweet warblings of the birds by the waterfall were mocking me. Not so long ago my darling heard these notes from our cottage and, calling me to listen, she would welcome the birds with much delight.

This fire—the spring—whose embers are the red clusters of the Aśoka tree, whose crackling and roaring are the hum of the bees, and whose flames are the young shoots, this fire will burn me up. What is life to me when I can no longer see my gentle-voiced Sītā of soft eyes and lovely hair? This vernal season when the trees blossom and re-echo with the cuckoo's notes was most dear to Sītā and my love for her will soon burn away my soul.[28]

[28] For the full details of this episode, see the Kiṣkindhya Kandam section of the *Rāmāyana*, Chapter I.

Rāma sees other beautiful scenes by Lake Pampā but they only serve to deepen his grief at the loss of Sītā. The joy and the love that he sees about him seem to mock his tragedy. The gentle spring wind inflames the fires of love and grief that burn within Rāma. All these things he has seen before, but with Sītā. To view alone those things which we shared with love—that indeed is pain.

## KĀMA AND ASPECTS OF ART

The sexual motif in the art and architecture of India is an expression of a dynamic aspect of life. This is true symbolically, philosophically, and empirically. The frank beauty of this sculpture is so bold as to be ingeniously pure. There is no room here for smutty jokes or crude laughter. Indeed there is humor, but it is the smile of spring and not the hollow guffaws of simpletons.

Carvings of couples in amorous poses exist in many sections of India. They have been found in Taxila (now located in Pakistan), Mathura, Bodh Gaya, Bhuvaneshwar, Varanasi, Puri, and Ellora, among other places. But the most famous are those at Konarak and Khajuraho. There have been a number of suggestions put forth to explain the existence of this erotic sculpture. Some believe that these carvings are to tempt those who visit the temples, but this seems to be a most unsatisfactory explanation and hardly accounts for the erotic sculpture hidden away in niches or in some obscure corner high on the temple. Another suggestion is that these carvings may symbolize certain philosophical principles of fertility and creation. Evidence certainly exists that may be interpreted to support this view, but it cannot explain the numerous sexual poses where no possibility of reproduction exists. Hardly anyone takes seriously the suggestion that this sculpture was an advertisement to induce male devotees to patronize the *devadāsīs* who bestowed their favors in the temple. That the sculpture was motivated through the caprice of the king desiring to gaze upon erotic poses is equally unsatisfactory as an explanation. Professor Basham puts forth the view that this temple sculpture represents the lower stages of heaven in which the sexual delights normally accessible only to kings and very wealthy men might at last be available to more ordinary folk. He remarks, "He was encouraged to hope for all the subtle refinements described in the *Kāma Sūtra,* which in our view, is far more relevant to the sculpture of Khajuraho and Konarak than is the literature of tantrism." [29] There is much to be said for this suggestion. Certainly many of the sexual positions described in the *Kāma Sūtra* are graphically depicted in the temple sculpture. The Sanskrit texts in a number of passages picture the joys of heaven, especially for Kṣatriyas fallen in battle, in terms of the sexual delights reserved for them there. That these temples, however, represent the palace of the king and suggest the nature of sexual activities there is doubtful, or at least probably not typical of the vast majority of ancient Indian rulers. Nevertheless, it remains that no explanation concerning the meaning and purpose of the erotic art and architecture of India has been recognized by scholars as entirely acceptable.

The temple at Konarak was built *ca.* A.D. 1255 and dedicated to Sūrya, the god of the sun. It was constructed to represent the chariot of Sūrya as he rides through the sky pulled by seven horses. The twelve pairs of wheels on which the temple seems to be mounted are ornamented with carvings of lovers and embracing couples. Floral de-

[29] *Journal of the Royal Asiatic Society,* Parts 1 and 2 (1960), p. 99.

signs, battle scenes, musicians, and animals also appear as part of the temple sculpture. The famous Konarak horse and wheel are often shown in works about Indian art. The temple today stands amidst ruins, and although some restoration has been attempted, much more is needed. The statue of Sūrya still stands on one of the higher levels of the Black Pagoda, as this temple is sometimes called. An impression of massive activity and majesty is conveyed by the sun temple at Konarak.

Khajuraho, the ancient capital of the Candellas in Bundelkhand, is today a small village living in the shadow of the most remarkable group of temples found anywhere in India. Of the eighty-five originally constructed between A.D. 950–1050, only twenty buildings remain. Some are in ruins. The Kandāriyā Mahādeva is the largest of those extant. It is over one hundred feet in length, sixty-six feet in width, and rises to a height above one hundred feet. Like many of the Khajuraho temples, it appears to be built in tiers with elaborate carvings covering practically all of the outside surface. There are nearly nine hundred images, many of which are about three feet high, on the walls of this temple. Gods, apsarases, serpents, lions, mythical beasts, and a large number of couples engaged in sexual activities are the main art motifs. There is a serenity that pervades the excitement depicted on these temples. Of the three main groups, western, eastern, and southern, the first series is the most famous. Although the sculptures are sometimes formal, they do not appear stiff or lifeless. When one has exhausted his vocabulary talking about beauty, exquisite charm, the wonders and techniques of art, the joys of life, and all the rest of it, there is still more to be said, which cannot be said, about Khajuraho.

### ASPECTS OF THE PHILOSOPHY OF *Kāma*

*Kāma* is not merely love, sensual desire, lust, affection, the name of a Hindu god, and so forth. It is also a philosophic principle and was considered as such from earliest times. We have already discussed *kāma* as one of the goals of life, and while that is surely a subject of philosophy, the idea of *kāma* extended much further than that. This is not to suggest that the *Kāma Sūtra* is a primary or even a significant work of philosophy. It is not. Vātsyāyana was no metaphysician delving into the religiophilosophical aspects of his subject. He does not even mention the temple dancing girls, much less a cosmic principle of unity. Nevertheless, the *Kāma Sūtra* is not without philosophical implications. The opinions that it expresses in the realm of morality and ethical conduct are significant not only in themselves but also as reflecting attitudes of the historical period in which it was written.

But what of the development of *kāma* as a principle of philosophy? Briefly, it is that through *kāma* one can obtain both unity and reality and, indeed, that unity and reality are the same. How does this express itself? *Kāma,* the principle of desire, was the source from which 'this creation and all creation began. Thus it was the One, the Beginning, and manifested itself in the many without destroying its own essence. It therefore became the universal factor of all things and the common link binding not only all mankind but all things whatsoever. Mankind is endlessly involved in the complexities of life. These are annoying, puzzling, and frustrating. He therefore seeks some common element which he is certain must connect all things and thus produce that security of unity for which he longs. What do you call that unifying force, that factor

upon which all else is based? Some call it God; others call
it Reality or the Absolute. One may attain or communicate
with Reality or the Absolute through the path of *kāma*,
which is both the source from which we came and the object to which we go. They mean the same. Love then becomes a yearning for union with the divinity. From this,
it is but a step to have the sex act itself considered as a
symbolic union in which the participants represent certain
cosmic principles. The power and the mystery of creation
is worshiped using the sexual organs as symbols. This idea
is not restricted to India in the history of religious thought,
although it reached a highly developed stage in the sub-
continent. The worship of the Śiva *liṅgam* in India today
pays obeisance to the creative aspect of that god's many
powers. The *bhaga* or *yoni* is and symbolizes the *śakti* or
the female creative principle.

In Mahāyāna Buddhism, these ideas were developed
further. Reality was achieved through the recognition that
plurality is unreal. The symbolism of Tibetan Yab-Yum
iconography (in which the male is in sexual embrace with
his Śakti or female counterpart) illustrates this thought.
The Śakti holds a knife and skull cup in her hands. The
knife symbolizes the destruction of ignorance while the
skull cup indicates absolute oneness. The sexual embrace
of the figures means that the distinction between duality
and non-duality is unreal and, as salt mixes into water, the
two beings mix themselves into one. All duality ceases and
only the one Reality remains. Tantric schools practiced
these activities as methods leading to liberation. Sensation-
alist writers have sometimes pictured the ceremony of these
groups as a wild sex orgy in which religious metaphysics
was merely an excuse for unrestrained debauchery. This is
absurd. As Zimmer remarks,

In spite of all the scandal that has been spread concerning this phase of Buddhist worship, the majority of the sacramental breaches (in a society hedged on every side by the most meticulous taboos) were not such as would give the slightest pause to the usual modern Christian gentleman or lady. They consisted in partaking of such forbidden foods as fish, meat, spicy dishes, and wine, and engaging in sexual intercourse. The sole novelty was that these acts were to be undertaken not in sensual eagerness or sated boredom, but without egoity and under the direction of a religious teacher, being regarded as concomitants of a difficult and dangerous yet absolutely indispensable spiritual exercise. The Bhodisattva is beyond desire and fear; moreover, all things are Buddha-things and void.[30]

But the philosophers of ancient India did not all look upon *kāma* or desire as something to be cherished. Lord Buddha saw it as the cause of all the misery and suffering in this world. Desire and attachment were millstones making it impossible for us to escape from the cycle of rebirths. The way to eliminate this suffering and rebirths was to eliminate desire and attachment. This was the principal theme of Gautama the Buddha. When he was sitting under the Bodhi tree at Bodh Gaya, it was Kāma who, in various forms, attempted to seduce him from Enlightenment. The Buddha resisted these temptations and spent the rest of his life in this world preaching against desire and attachment as things conducive only to suffering and never to enlightenment. The *Mahābhārata* and other texts contain similar views. The *Bhāgavad Gītā*, that much overworked source of Hinduism, says that the fruit of *kāma* is pain and ignorance is the fruit of laziness. *Kāma* tastes

[30] H. Zimmer, *Philosophies of India,* pp. 554-55. This excellent work by one of the most reputable Indologists is now available in paperback from Meridian Books (MG 6), New York, 1956.

like honey, but in reality it is poison. The texts of Hinduism are like an ocean in which many fish live that devour each other.

## MARRIAGE AND THE *Kāma Sūtra*

What has been written above is largely background material which may help us to understand some of the attitudes of ancient India in relation to *kāma*. Whatever the metaphysical or legendary implications were, society rigorously anathemized most sexual activity for the ordinary citizen outside the bonds of marriage. This attitude has persisted in India to the present time. Marriage was not merely an expression of *kāma;* it was a sacred duty. The idea of permanent celibacy was intolerable.

The great ascetic Jaratkāru had wandered all over the earth living only on air and bathing in various sacred waters, free of all worldly desires. One day he came across a pit in which he saw his ancestors in a starved and miserable condition. They were holding onto the side of the pit by a single creeper. Below them snakes and horrible animals were waiting to devour them when they fell. As they were holding onto the creeper fearful of the horrors below, a tiny rat was gnawing away that last thread of safety. Jaratkāru was filled with pity at seeing his ancestors in such a plight and offered to redeem them even if it meant losing all of his immense ascetic powers. They replied that they also had ascetic powers, but such things were powerless in their situation. The pit represented hell; the creeper, their last hope, represented the possibility of Jaratkāru having a son that would offer worship to save them; and the rat was time. Not recognizing Jaratkāru, they told him that if the pious ascetic should see their descendant he should be told that it was through his fault they were suffering. Because he had no wife or son or relatives, they had come to this condition. Asceticism, sacrifices, and holy acts were nothing compared with the birth of a son. Upon hearing these words, Jaratkāru wept and resolved to marry, thus putting an end to his own and his ancestors' suffering.[31]

Basically there were three purposes for marriage. By producing children the father and ancestors were assured of a pleasant future life through the sacrifices that would be offered to them. Otherwise they were doomed to misery. Marriage also helped to promote religious objectives, not only because it was one of the twelve Saṃskāras or sacraments, but also because of the religious duties required of a householder.[32] The third objective of marriage was the proper fulfillment of sexual pleasures. We have already seen how important this was considered in India. It was to help achieve this objective of marriage that the *Kāma Sūtra* was written.

Evaluated from this point of view alone, the *Kāma Sūtra* offers much advice that would be of value in promoting happy marriages throughout the world. How many women are proficient in even half of the sixty-four arts

[31] This tale comes from the *Mahābhārata,* Adi Parvan, Section 40*ff*. It is repeated with variations in other sources.

[32] The five great acts of worship or *Mahāyajnas* were: (1) worship of Brāhman by recitation of the Veda; (2) worship of the Pitṛs or departed ancestors by daily offerings of water and special ceremonies; (3) worship of the gods; (4) worship of all beings by providing food for animals and spirits; and (5) hospitality toward guests. The last is not an act of "charity," as it is sometimes considered in the West, but rather a guest gives the householder an opportunity to perform a religious act by showing kindness. This view is still held in parts of India today and a visitor to that country is the recipient of extraordinary kindness and hospitality such as I have seldom seen in any other part of the world.

suggested for study by Vātsyāyana? Even if we disregard certain magical aspects, there is much to be said for paying some attention to the qualities that the *Kāma Sūtra* suggests are desirable in a wife. Observe the wealth of understanding and tenderness that our author shows when he discusses the methods of creating confidence in the new bride. And what a tragedy it is that ignorance of these approaches, rather than stupidity, has led so many women to the psychiatrist's office or the divorce court. Read in this book also about the conduct which a woman should follow when her husband is absent. But you may say Vātsyāyana was a prude in such matters. He was neither one extreme nor the other. He was a social scientist in the best sense of the word who attempted to use his knowledge and experience for the happiness and betterment of mankind. There is no vulgarity in what he has written, nor should there be in what you read. Vātsyāyana was eminently a moralist, whether or not one agrees with what he has to say. Probably the most ancient marriage manual in existence is now in your hands. You cannot but be impressed, in spite of his magical charms or naïveté, with his understanding of human nature and the applicability of what is said to modern times.

## THE *Kāma Sūtra* AS A HISTORICAL DOCUMENT

Indologists, historians, and other scholars have found the *Kāma Sūtra* a valuable source of evidence in their various academic disciplines, for one of the major problems in Indology is the paucity of evidence with which we must deal. As Professor Basham put it,

We can learn much about the life of the Greek and Roman bourgeoisie from literature and archaeological remains; but the comparable literature of India was less realistic, and there is no Indian counterpart of Pompeii. Nevertheless there is enough evidence to reconstruct the life of the well-to-do young Indian in some detail from secular literature, one of our most important sources being the treatise on erotics, the *Kāma Sūtra,* which was composed to instruct him in one of his chief recreations.[33]

Chapter IV of Part One indicates what some of these diversions were. Indian festivals are nearly always an occasion for holiday making and in Varanāsi (Benares) today there are more festivals than there are days in the year. Vātsyāyana suggests that a group of citizens may gather at the temple of Sarasvatī and listen to musical performances both as an amusement and as a form of worship to this goddess of music, arts, and learning.[34] Pleasant conversation among men and women of similar tastes was also a form of recreation. The *Kāma Sūtra* suggests that such women were courtesans, and we may imply from this that the free mingling of the sexes was not encouraged, and indeed probably severely restricted, during this period of India's history. Drinking parties, picnics, animal fights, swimming or playing in the water, and gambling were among other forms of recreation suggested by Vātsyāyana. From his remarks, we can observe not only the manner of life of some of the upper classes in ancient India, but also the changes that have taken place as one views Indian

[33] A. L. Basham, *The Wonder That Was India* (London: Sidgwick and Jackson, 1954), p. 205.

[34] The evolution of the goddess Sarasvatī in Hindu mythology is still unclear. This passage indicates that at least by the time of the writing of the *Kāma Sūtra,* Sarasvatī was established as the goddess of music. That there were temples dedicated especially to her suggests a considerable popular following at this time. While Sarasvatī is still the goddess of music today, her position as goddess of learning is probably more dominant.

society today. This text is also of value in determining the evolution of ancient Indian thought. For example, both the *Arthaśāstra* of Kauṭilya and the *Kāma Sūtra* mention lists of kings that were victims of various kinds of intrigues and their list of the *trivarga* is identical. At the same time, there is considerable difference in their respective attitudes toward eating meat and the influence of stars. The recipes and charms for aphrodisiacs given in the *Kāma Sūtra* show a development from a long list given in the *Atharva Veda*. The ideal of feminine beauty given in the *Kāma Sūtra* allows us not only to make comparisons with other Indian texts, but also to see the differences between the Indian ideal and those of countries in the Western world. We are still largely ignorant about the status and education of women in ancient India, and there is much room for research on this subject. The *Kāma Sūtra* prescribes a number of different subjects for women to study, and we may deduce that whatever decline took place in female education occurred after the writing of the *Kāma Sūtra*. Nevertheless, this work itself must have been a beneficial force influencing Indian education.

The sociological evidence contained in the *Kāma Sūtra* is of the utmost significance. In the matter of divorce, it confirms other evidence which says that a marriage celebrated with the sacred fire as witness cannot be revoked. The various types of legitimate marriage are also discussed in this text and interesting comparisons can be made with the statements given in *Manu* and other *Dharmaśāstra* texts. Even when there is an inconsistency, such as when the *Kāma Sūtra* declares in one place that the Brāhma type of marriage is to be preferred and in another that the Gāndharva is most desirable, this also helps us in determining the possible rigidity of the system then operating.

The information relating to the selection of a bride given by Vātsyāyana is also useful. Indeed, some of the factors mentioned by him continue to influence Indian marriage customs up to the present day. We can also trace the development of some of these ideas from earlier times, as they appear in the *Śatapatha Brāhmaṇa,* for example, to the variations described in the *Kāma Sūtra.* The problem of child marriage has been especially controversial in modern Indian history. Was child marriage, as some suggest, a Hindu reaction against the Muslim conquest or is it advocated by the ancient texts and if so, to what extent? Again, the *Kāma Sūtra* as a historical document provides us with useful information. This text also tells us something about *satī* or widow burning.

In the study of ancient Indian political ideas and institutions we are aided by the evidence in the *Kāma Sūtra.* It is significant that many of the political officers mentioned by Kauṭilya in Book Two of the *Arthaśāstra* also appear under the same names in the *Kāma Sūtra.* The life of a king in ancient India was somewhat limited by his responsibilities. Many of the texts narrate legends or tell us the theoretical position of the king. Very few sources give us much of the actual historical realities. Vātsyāyana tells us of the dangers that kings faced and, indeed, how some of them fell. He lists certain kings about whom we know very little, and should further evidence become available about these personages, the statements of the *Kāma Sūtra* might help us considerably. The influence of various government officials, which is mentioned by Vātsyāyana, helps us reconstruct some aspects of governmental administration and ascertains, to some extent, the actual powers of the king. The influence of the *grāmādhipati* (the lord of the village) may help indicate the extent of village or local political autonomy in ancient India.

This is only part of the evidence which we may obtain from the *Kāma Sūtra,* using it as a historical document. Social taboos, names of tribes and peoples, prevailing customs and attitudes in various parts of the country, local prejudices, and economic aspects could all be added and discussed. The important consideration is that *The Kāma Sūtra of Vātsyāyana* is a valuable work from many points of view. It is certainly a classic and deserves far more respect and understanding than it has heretofore received in the West.

The translation used in this volume was done by Sir Richard F. Burton in 1838 for the Kāma Sāstra Society of London and Benares. It was privately printed and sold and subsequently pirated for other editions. Sanskritists will certainly find a number of places where they differ with the interpretation that Burton has given. For highly specialized Indological studies, this translation is not considered dependable, but in such cases the scholar will, of course, consult the work in the original Sanskrit. The lack of diacritical marks also takes away some of the luster of this publication. Nevertheless, there is much to commend. We now have in this country an English translation of this work which is publicly available for students and others interested in aspects of ancient Indian civilization. This is a very great step forward and one for which we should be thankful.

I have given above some of the ways in which the *Kāma Sūtra* has affected and been affected by Indian civilization and Hindu concepts. In these aspects the work is of profound importance to students all over the world. But this classic is not merely a historical text or something of interest to Indologists alone. For many it will provide a new horizon with which to enrich their experiences in this life. The style of Vātsyāyana makes this book a joy to read and his poetic manner, sympathetic understanding, and even his stern moral injunctions make us feel that there is nothing distant or lifeless in his remarks. Although no politician, he has something worth while to offer nearly everyone. For those of us who have read this book there is always a delight in rereading it. For those of us who have not, I am glad to introduce to you one of the greatest classics of all time. For those of us who will not—*honi soit qui mal y pense.*

JOHN W. SPELLMAN

*Ashburnham, Mass.*

# THE
# KAMA SUTRA
# OF
# VATSYAYANA

# INTRODUCTORY PREFACE

*Salutation to Dharma, Artha, and Kama*

In the beginning the Lord of Beings (Brahma) created men and women, and in the form of commandments in one hundred thousand chapters laid down rules for regulating their existence with regard to Dharma,[1] Artha,[2] and Kama.[3] Some

These three words are retained throughout in their original, as technical terms. They may also be defined as virtue, wealth, and pleasure, the three things repeatedly spoken of in the Laws of Manu.

of these commandments, namely, those which treated of Dharma, were separately written by Swayambhu Manu; those that related to Artha were compiled by Brihaspati; and those that referred to Kama were expounded by Nandi, the follower of Mahadeva, in one thousand chapters.

Now, these *Kama Sutra* (Aphorisms on Love), written by Nandi in one thousand chapters, were reproduced by Shvetaketu, the son of Uddvalaka, in an abbreviated form in five hundred chapters, and this work was again similarly reproduced in an abridged form, in one hundred and fifty chapters, by Babhravya, an inhabitant of the Panchala (South of Delhi) country. These one hundred and fifty chapters were then put together under seven heads or parts named severally:

1. Sadharana (general topics)
2. Samprayogika (embraces, and so on)

[1] Dharma is acquisition of religious merit, and is fully described in Chapter 5, Volume III, of James Talboys Wheeler's *History of India*, and in the edicts of Asoka.

[2] Artha is acquisition of wealth and property, etc.

[3] Kama is love, pleasure, and sensual gratification.

3. Kanya Samprayuktaka (union of males and females)
4. Bharyadhikarika (on one's own wife)
5. Paradarika (on the wives of other people)
6. Vaisika (on courtesans)
7. Aupamishadika (on the arts of seduction, tonic medicines, and so on)

The sixth part of this last work was separately expounded by Dattaka at the request of the public women of Pataliputra (Patna), and in the same way Charayana explained the first part of it. The remaining parts, namely, the second, third, fourth, fifth, and seventh, were separately expounded by:

Suvarnanabha (second part).
Ghotakamukha (third part).
Gonardiya (fourth part).
Gonikaputra (fifth part).
Kuchumara (seventh part).

Thus the work, being written in parts by different authors, was almost unobtainable, and as the parts which were expounded by Dattaka and the others treated only of the particular branches of the subject to which each part related, and moreover as the original work of Babhravya was difficult to be mastered on account of its length, Vatsyayana composed this work in a small volume as an abstract of the whole of the works of the above-named authors.

# PART ONE

*Society and Social Concepts*

## Chapter I

### Being the Index to or Contents of the Work

### PART TWO: On Sexual Union

## PART THREE: *About the Acquisition of a Wife*

## PART FOUR: *About a Wife*

## PART FIVE: *About the Wives of Other Men*

---

## PART SIX: *About Courtesans*

---

## PART SEVEN: *On the Means of Attracting Others to Yourself*

---

I   On personal adornment, subjugating the hearts of others, and on tonic medicines

II  On the means of exciting desire, and of the ways of enlarging the lingam. Miscellaneous experiments and recipes.

## Chapter II

### On the Acquisition of Dharma, Artha, and Kama

Man, the period of whose life is one hundred years, should practice Dharma, Artha, and Kama at different times and in such a manner that they may harmonize, and not clash in any way. He should acquire learning in his childhood; in his youth and middle age he should attend to Artha and Kama; and in his old age he should perform Dharma, and thus seek to gain Moksha, that is, release from further transmigration. Or, because of the uncertainty of life, he may practice them at times when they are enjoined to be practiced. But one thing is to be noted: he should lead the life of a religious student until he finishes his education.

*Dharma* is obedience to the command of the Shastra, or Holy Writ, of the Hindus to do certain things, such as the performance of sacrifices, which are not generally done because they do not belong to this world, and produce no visible effect; and not do other things, such as eating meat, which is often done because it belongs to this world, and has visible effects.

Dharma should be learned from the Shruti (Holy Writ), and from those conversant with it.

*Artha* is the acquisition of arts, land, gold, cattle, wealth, equipages, and friends. It is also the protection of what is acquired, and the increase of what is protected.

Artha should be learned from the king's officers, and from merchants who may be versed in the ways of commerce.

63

*Kama* is the enjoyment of appropriate objects by the five senses of hearing, feeling, seeing, tasting, and smelling, assisted by the mind together with the soul. The ingredient in this is a peculiar contact between the organ of sense and its object, and the consciousness of pleasure that arises from that contact is called Kama.

Kama is to be learned from the *Kama Sutra* (aphorisms on love) and the practice of citizens.

When all three, Dharma, Artha, and Kama, come together, the former is better than the one which follows it; that is, Dharma is better than Artha, and Artha is better than Kama. But Artha should always be first practiced by the king, for the livelihood of men is to be obtained from it only. Again, Kama being the occupation of public women, they should prefer it to the other two, and these are exceptions to the general rule.

### Objection

Some learned men say that as Dharma is connected with things not belonging to this world, it is appropriately treated of in a book; and so also is Artha, because it is practiced only by the application of proper means, and a knowledge of those means can be obtained only by study and from books. But Kama being a thing which is practiced even by the brute creation, and which is to be found everywhere, does not want any work on the subject.

### Answer

This is not so. Sexual intercourse, being a thing dependent on man and woman, requires the application of proper means by them, and those means are to be learned from the *Kama Shastra*. The nonapplication of proper means, which we see in the brute creation, is caused by their being unrestrained, and by the females among them being fit for sexual intercourse at certain seasons only and no more, and by their intercourse not being preceded by thought of any kind.

*Objection*

The Lokayatikas [1] say: Religious ordinances should not be observed, for they bear a future fruit, and at the same time it is also doubtful whether they will bear any fruit at all. What foolish person will give away that which is in his own hands into the hands of another? Moreover, it is better to have a pigeon today than a peacock tomorrow; and a copper coin we have the certainty of obtaining is better than a gold coin the possession of which is doubtful.

*Answer*

It is not so. First, Holy Writ, which ordains the practice of Dharma, does not admit of a doubt.

Second, sacrifices such as those made for the destruction of enemies, or for the fall of rain, are seen to bear fruit.

Third, the sun, moon, stars, planets, and other heavenly bodies appear to work intentionally for the good of the world.

Fourth, the existence of this world is effected by the observance of the rules respecting the four classes [2] of men and their four stages of life.

Fifth, we see that seed is thrown into the ground with the hope of future crops.

Vatsyayana is therefore of the opinion that the ordinances of religion must be obeyed.

*Objection*

Those who believe that destiny is the prime mover of all things say: We should not exert ourselves to acquire wealth, for sometimes it is not acquired although we strive to get it,

[1] These were certainly materialists who seemed to think that a bird in the hand was worth two in the bush.

[2] Among the Hindus the four classes of men are the Brahmans, or priestly class; the Kshatriyas, or warrior class; the Vaishya, or agricultural and mercantile class; and the Shudra, or menial class. The four stages of life are: the life of a religious student (Brahmacarin), the life of the householder (Grihastha), the life of a Vana prastha, or forest dweller, and the life of a Sannyas, or wandering ascetic.

while at other times it comes to us of itself without any exertion on our part. Everything is therefore in the power of destiny, who is the lord of gain and loss, of success and defeat, of pleasure and pain. Thus we see that Bali [3] was raised to the throne of Indra by destiny, and was also put down by the same power, and only destiny can reinstate him.

### Answer

It is not right to say so. As the acquisition of every object presupposes at all events some exertion on the part of man, the application of proper means may be said to be the cause of gaining all our ends, and this application of proper means being thus necessary (even where a thing is destined to happen), it follows that a person who does nothing will enjoy no happiness.

### Objection

Those who are inclined to think that Artha is the chief object to be obtained argue thus: Pleasures should not be sought for, because they are obstacles to the practice of Dharma and Artha, which are both superior to them, and are also disliked by meritorious persons. Pleasures also bring a man into distress, and into contact with low persons; they cause him to commit unrighteous deeds, and produce impurity in him; they make him regardless of the future, and encourage carelessness and levity. And, lastly, they cause him to be disbelieved by all, received by none, and despised by everybody, including himself. It is notorious, moreover, that many men who have given themselves up to pleasure alone have been ruined along with their families and relations. Thus King Dandakya,[4] of the Bhoja dynasty, carried off a Brahman's

[3] Bali was a demon who had conquered Indra and gained his throne, but was afterward overcome by Vishnu at the time of his fifth incarnation.

[4] Dandakya is said to have abducted from the forest the daughter of a Brahman, named Bhargava, and being cursed by the Brahman, was buried with his kingdom under a shower of dust. The place was

daughter with evil intent, and was eventually ruined and lost
his kingdom. Indra, too, having violated the chastity of
Ahalya,[5] was made to suffer for it. In like manner the
mighty Kichaka,[6] who tried to seduce Draupadi; and Ravana,[7]
who attempted to gain over Sita, were punished for their
crimes. These and many others fell by reason of their pleasures.

### Answer

This objection cannot be sustained, for pleasures, being as
necessary for the existence and well-being of the body as
food, are consequently equally required. They are, moreover,
the results of Dharma and Artha. Pleasures are, therefore, to
be followed with moderation and caution. No one refrains
from cooking food because there are beggars to ask for it,
or from sowing seed because there are deer to destroy the corn
when it has grown up.

Thus a man practicing Dharma, Artha, and Kama enjoys
happiness both in this world and in the world to come. The
good perform those actions in which there is no fear as to
what is to result from them in the next world, and in which
there is no danger to their welfare. Any action which conduces
to the practice of Dharma, Artha, and Kama together, or of
any two, or even of one of them, should be performed, but an
action which conduces to the practice of one of them at the
expense of the remaining two should not be performed.

---

called after his name the Dandaka Forest, celebrated in the Ramayana,
but now unknown.

[5] Ahalya was the wife of the sage Gautama. Indra caused her to
believe that he was Gautama, and thus enjoyed her. He was cursed by
Gautama and subsequently afflicted with a thousand ulcers on his
body.

[6] Kichaka was the brother-in-law of King Virata, with whom the
Pandavas had taken refuge for one year. Kichaka was killed by Bhima,
who assumed the disguise of Draupadi. For this story the Mahabharata
should be referred to.

[7] The story of Ravana is told in the Ramayana; the Ramayana and
the Mahabharata are the two great epic poems of the Hindus; the
latter was written by Vyasa, and the former by Vlamiki.

## Chapter III

### On the Arts and Sciences to Be Studied

Man should study the *Kama Sutra* and the arts and sciences subordinate thereto, in addition to the study of the arts and sciences contained in Dharma and Artha. Even young maids should study this *Kama Sutra*, along with its arts and sciences, before marriage, and after it they should continue to do so with the consent of their husbands.

Here some learned men object, and say that females, not being allowed to study any science, should not study the *Kama Sutra*.

But Vatsyayana is of opinion that this objection does not hold good, for women already know the practice of *Kama Sutra*, and that practice is derived from the *Kama Shastra*, or the science of Kama itself. Moreover, it is not only in this but in many other cases that, though the practice of a science is known to all, only a few persons are acquainted with the rules and laws on which the science is based. Thus the Yajnikas, or sacrificers, though ignorant of grammar, make use of appropriate words when addressing the different deities, and do not know how these words are framed. Again, persons do the duties required of them on auspicious days, which are fixed by astrology, though they are not acquainted with the science of astrology. In a like manner riders of horses and elephants train these animals without knowing the science of training animals, but from practice only. And similarly the people of the most distant provinces obey the laws of the kingdom from practice, and because there is a king over them, and without further reason.[1] And from experience we find that some women, such as the daughters of princes and their ministers, and public women, are actually versed in the *Kama Shastra*.

A female, therefore, should learn the *Kama Shastra*, or at least a part of it, by studying its practice from some confidential friend. She should study alone, in private, the sixty-four practices that form a part of the *Kama Shastra*. Her teacher should be one of the following persons; namely, the daughter of a nurse brought up with her and already married,[2] or a female friend who can be trusted in everything, or the sister of her mother (that is, her aunt), or an old female servant, or a female beggar who may have formerly lived in the family, or her own sister, who can always be trusted.

The following are the arts to be studied, together with the *Kama Sutra*:

1. Singing.
2. Playing on musical instruments.
3. Dancing.
4. Union of dancing, singing, and playing instrumental music.
5. Writing and drawing.
6. Tattooing.
7. Arraying and adorning an idol with rice and flowers.
8. Spreading and arranging beds or couches of flowers, or flowers upon the ground.
9. Coloring the teeth, garments, hair, nails and bodies, that is, staining, dyeing, coloring, and painting them.
10. Fixing stained glass into a floor.

[1] The author wishes to prove that a great many things are done by people from practice and custom, without their being acquainted with the reason of things, or the laws on which they are based, and this is perfectly true.

[2] The proviso of being married applies to all the teachers.

11. The art of making beds, and spreading out carpets and cushions for reclining.

12. Playing on musical glasses filled with water.

13. Storing and accumulating water in aqueducts, cisterns, and reservoirs.

14. Picture making, trimming and decorating.

15. Stringing of rosaries, necklaces, garlands, and wreaths.

16. Binding of turbans and chaplets, and making crests and topknots of flowers.

17. Scenic representations. Stage playing.

18. Art of making ear ornaments.

19. Art of preparing perfumes and odors.

20. Proper disposition of jewels and decorations, and adornment in dress.

21. Magic or sorcery.

22. Quickness and dexterity in manual skill.

23. Culinary art, that is, cooking and cookery.

24. Making lemonades, sherbets, acidulated drinks, and spirituous extracts with proper flavor and color.

25. Tailor's work and sewing.

26. Making parrots, flowers, tufts, tassels, bunches, bosses, knobs, and so on, out of yarn or thread.

27. Solution of riddles, enigmas, covert speeches, verbal puzzles, and enigmatical questions.

28. A game, which consists in repeating verses, and as one person finishes, another person has to commence at once, repeating another verse, beginning with the same letter with which the last speaker's verse ended. Whoever fails to repeat, is considered to have lost and to be subject to pay a forfeit or stake of some kind.

29. The art of mimicry or imitation.

30. Reading, including chanting and intoning.

31. Study of sentences difficult to pronounce. It is played as a game, chiefly by women and children, and consists of a difficult sentence being given; and when it is repeated quickly, the words are often transposed or badly pronounced.

32. Practice with sword, single-stick, quarterstaff, and bow and arrow.

33. Drawing inferences, reasoning or inferring.

34. Carpentry, or the work of a carpenter.

35. Architecture, or the art of building.

36. Knowledge about gold and silver coins, and jewels and gems.

37. Chemistry and mineralogy.

38. Coloring jewels, gems, and beads.

39. Knowledge of mines and quarries.

40. Gardening; knowledge of treating the diseases of trees and plants, of nourishing them, and determining their ages.

41. Arts of cockfighting, quail fighting, and ram fighting.

42. Art of teaching parrots and starlings to speak.

43. Art of applying perfumed ointments to the body, and of dressing the hair with unguents and perfumes, and braiding it.

44. The art of understanding writing in cipher and the writing of words in a peculiar way.

45. The art of speaking by changing the forms of words. It is of various kinds. Some speak by changing the beginning and end of words, others by adding unnecessary letters between every syllable of a word, and so on.

46. Knowledge of languages and of the vernacular dialects.

47. Art of making flower carriages.

48. Art of framing mystical diagrams, of addressing spells and charms, and binding armlets.

49. Mental exercises, such as completing stanzas or verses on receiving a part of them; or supplying one, two, or three lines when the remaining lines are given indiscriminately from different verses, so as to make the whole an entire verse with regard to its meaning; or arranging the words of a verse written irregularly by separating the vowels from the consonants, or leaving them out altogether; or putting into verse or prose sentences represented by signs or symbols. There are many other such exercises.

50. Composing poems.

51. Knowledge of dictionaries and vocabularies.

52. Knowledge of ways of changing and disguising the appearance of persons.

53. Knowledge of the art of changing the appearance of things, such as making cotton to appear as silk, coarse and common things to appear as fine and good.

54. Various ways of gambling.

55. Art of obtaining possession of the property of others by means of muntras or incantations.

56. Skill in youthful sports.

57. Knowledge of the rules of society, and of how to pay respects and compliments to others.

58. Knowledge of the art of war, of arms, armies, and so on.

59. Knowledge of gymnastics.

60. Art of knowing the character of a man from his features.

61. Knowledge of scanning or constructing verses.

62. Arithmetical recreations.

63. Making artificial flowers.

64. Making figures and images in clay.

A public woman, endowed with a good disposition, beauty, and other winning qualities, and also versed in the above arts, obtains the name of a Ganika, or public woman of high quality, and receives a seat of honor in an assemblage of men. She is, moreover, always respected by the king, and praised by learned men, and her favor being sought for by all, she becomes an object of universal regard. The daughter of a king, too, as well as the daughter of a minister, being learned in the above arts, can make their husbands favorable to them, even though these may have thousands of other wives besides themselves. And in the same manner, if a wife becomes separated from her husband, and falls into distress, she can support herself easily, even in a foreign country, by means of her knowledge of these arts. Even the bare knowledge of them gives attractiveness to a woman, though the practice of them may be possible only according to the circumstances of each case. A man who is versed in these arts, who is loquacious and acquainted with the arts of gallantry, gains very soon the hearts of women, even though he is acquainted with them for only a short time.

## Chapter IV

### The Life of the Citizen [1]

Having thus acquired learning, a man, with the wealth that he may have gained by gift, conquest, purchase, deposit,[2] or inheritance from his ancestors, should become a householder (Grihastha), and pass the life of a citizen. He should take a house in a city or large village, or in the vicinity of good men, or in a place which is the resort of many persons. This abode should be situated near some water, and divided into different compartments for different purposes. It should be surrounded by a garden, and also contain two rooms, an outer and an inner one. The inner room should be occupied by the females, while the outer room, balmy with rich perfumes, should contain a bed, soft, agreeable to the sight, covered with a clean white cloth, low in the middle part, having garlands and bunches of flowers [3] upon it, and a canopy above it, and two pillows, one at the top, another at the bottom. There should be also a sort of couch, and at the head of this a sort of stool, on which should be placed the fragrant ointments for the night, such as flowers, pots containing collyrium and other fragrant

[1] This term would appear to apply generally to an inhabitant of Hindustan. It is not meant only for a dweller in a city, like the Latin Urbanus as opposed to Rusticus.

[2] Gift is peculiar to a Brahman, conquest to a Kshatriya, while purchase, deposit, and other means of acquiring wealth belong to the Vaishya.

[3] Natural garden flowers.

substances, things used for perfuming the mouth, and the bark of the common citron tree. Near the couch, on the ground, there should be a pot for spitting, a box containing ornaments, and also a lute hanging from a peg made of the tooth of an elephant, a board for drawing, a pot containing perfume, some books, and some garlands of the yellow amaranth flowers. Not far from the couch, and on the ground, there should be a round seat, a toy cart, and a board for playing with dice; outside the outer room there should be cages of birds,[4] and a separate place for spinning, carving and such-like diversions. In the garden there should be a whirling swing and a common swing, as well as a bower of creepers covered with flowers, in which a raised parterre should be made for sitting.

Now, the householder, having got up in the morning and performed his necessary duties,[5] should wash his teeth, apply a limited quantity of ointments and perfumes to his body, put some ornaments on his person and collyrium on his eyelids and below his eyes, color his lips with alacktaka,[6] and look at himself in the glass. Having then eaten betel leaves, with other things that give fragrance to the mouth, he should perform his usual business. He should bathe daily, anoint his body with oil every other day, apply a lathering [7] substance to his body every three days, get his head (including face) shaved every four days and the other parts of his body every five or ten days.[8] All these things should be done without fail, and the sweat of the armpits should also be removed. Meals should be taken in the forenoon, in the afternoon, and again at night, according to Charayana. After breakfast, parrots

[4] Such as quails, partridges, parrots, starlings, etc.

[5] The calls of nature are always performed by the Hindus the first thing in the morning.

[6] A color made from lac.

[7] This would act instead of soap, which was not introduced until the rule of the Muslims.

[8] Ten days are allowed when the hair is taken out with a pair of pincers.

and other birds should be taught to speak, and the fighting of cocks, quails, and rams should follow. A limited time should be devoted to diversions with Pithamardas, Vitas, and Vidushakas,[9] and then the midday sleep should be taken.[10] After this, the householder, having put on his clothes and ornaments, should, during the afternoon, converse with his friends. In the evening there should be singing, and after that the householder, along with his friend, should await in his room, previously decorated and perfumed, the arrival of the woman that may be attached to him, or he may send a female messenger for her or go to her himself. After her arrival at his house, he and his friends should welcome her and entertain her with a loving and agreeable conversation. Thus end the duties of the day.

The following are the things to be done occasionally as diversions or amusements:

1. Holding festival [11] in honor of different deities
2. Social gatherings of both sexes
3. Drinking parties
4. Picnics
5. Other social diversions

*Festivals*

On some particularly auspicious day, an assembly of citizens should be convened in the temple of Saraswati.[12] There the skill of singers, and of others who may have come

[9] These are characters generally introduced in the Hindu drama; their characteristics will be explained further on.

[10] Noonday sleep is allowed only in summer, when the nights are short.

[11] These are very common in all parts of India.

[12] In the *Asiatic Miscellany,* and in Sir William Jones's works, will be found a spirited hymn addressed to this goddess, who is adored as the patroness of the fine arts, especially of music and rhetoric, as the inventress of the Sanskrit language, etc. She is the goddess of harmony, eloquence, and language, and is somewhat analogous to Minerva. For further information about her see Edward Moor's *The Hindoo Pantheon.*

recently to the town, should be tested, and on the following day they should always be given some rewards. After that, they may either be retained or dismissed, according as their performances are liked or not by the assembly. The members of the assembly should act in concert both in times of distress as well as in times of prosperity, and it is also the duty of these citizens to show hospitality to strangers who may have come to the assembly. What is said above should be understood to apply to all the other festivals which may be held in honor of the different deities according to the present rules.

## Social Gatherings

When men of the same age, disposition, and talents, fond of the same diversions and with the same degree of education, sit together in company with public women,[13] or in an assembly of citizens, or at the abode of one among themselves, and engage in agreeable discourse with each other, such is called a sitting in company or a social gathering. The subjects of discourse are to be the completion of verses half composed by others, and the testing of the knowledge of one another in the various arts. The women who may be the most beautiful, who may like the same things that the men like, and who may have power to attract the minds of others, are here done homage to.

[13] The public women, or courtesans (Vesya), of the early Hindus have often been compared with the Hetera of the Greeks. The subject is dealt with at some length in H. H. Wilson's *Select Specimens of the Theatre of the Hindoos,* in two volumes (Trübner and Co., 1871). It may be fairly considered that the courtesan was one of the elements, and an important element too, of early Hindu society, and that her education and intellect were both superior to that of the women of the household. Wilson says: "By the Vesya or courtesan, however, we are not to understand a female who has disregarded the obligation of law or the precepts of virtue, but a character reared by a state of manners unfriendly to the admission of wedded females into society, and opening it only at the expense of reputation to women who were trained for association with men by personal and mental acquirements to which the matron was a stranger."

## Drinking Parties

Men and women should drink in one another's houses. And here the men should cause the public women to drink, and should then drink themselves, liquors such as the Madhu, Aireya, Sura, and Asawa, which are of bitter and sour taste; also drinks concocted from the barks of various trees, wild fruits, and leaves.

## Going to Gardens or Picnics

In the forenoon, men, having dressed themselves, should go to gardens on horseback, accompanied by public women and followed by servants. And having done there all the duties of the day, and passed the time in various agreeable diversions, such as the fighting of quails, cocks, and rams, and other spectacles, they should return home in the afternoon in the same manner, bringing with them bunches of flowers, and so on.

The same also applies to bathing in summer in water from which poisonous or dangerous animals have previously been taken out, and which has been built in on all sides.

## Other Social Diversions

Spending nights playing with dice. Going out on moonlight nights. Keeping the festive day in honor of spring. Plucking the sprouts and fruits of the mango trees. Eating the fibers of lotuses. Eating the tender ears of corn. Picniking in the forests when the trees get their new foliage. The Udakakshvedika, or sporting in the water. Decorating each other with the flowers of some trees. Pelting each other with the flowers of the Kadamba tree, and many other sports which may either be known to the whole country or may be peculiar to particular parts of it. These and similar amusements should always be carried on by citizens.

The above amusements should be followed by a person who diverts himself alone in company with a courtesan, as well as by a courtesan who can do the same in company with her maidservants or with citizens.

A Pithamarda [14] is a man without wealth, alone in the world, whose only property consists of his Mallika,[15] some lathering substance, and a red cloth, who comes from a good country, and who is skilled in all the arts; and by teaching these arts is received in the company of citizens, and in the abode of public women.

A Vita [16] is a man who has enjoyed the pleasures of fortune, who is a compatriot of the citizens with whom he associates, who is possessed of the qualities of a householder, who has his wife with him, and who is honored in the assembly of citizens and in the abodes of public women, and lives on their means and on them.

A Vidushaka [17] (also called a Vaihasaka, that is, one who provokes laughter) is a person acquainted with only some of the arts, who is a jester, and who is trusted by all.

These persons are employed in matters of quarrels and reconciliations between citizens and public women. This remark applies also to female beggars, to women with their

[14] According to this description a Pithamarda would be a sort of professor of all the arts, and as such received as the friend and confidant of the citizens.

[15] A seat in the form of the letter $T$.

[16] The Vita is supposed to represent somewhat the character of the Parasite of the Greek comedy. It is possible that he was retained about the person of the wealthy, and employed as a kind of private instructor, as well as an entertaining companion.

[17] Vidushaka is evidently the buffoon and jester. Wilson says of him that he is the humble companion, not the servant, of a prince or man of rank, and it is a curious peculiarity that he is always a Brahman. He bears more affinity to Sancho Panza, perhaps, than any other character in Western fiction, imitating him in his combination of shrewdness and simplicity, his fondness of good living and his love of ease. In the dramas of intrigue he exhibits some of the talents of Mercury, but with less activity and ingenuity, and occasionally suffers by his interference. According to the technical definition of his attributes he is to excite mirth by being ridiculous in person, age, and attire.

heads shaven, to adulterous women, and to old public women skilled in all the various arts.

Thus a citizen living in his town or village, respected by all, should call on the persons of his own caste who may be worth knowing. He should converse in company and gratify his friends by his society; and obliging others by his assistance in various matters, he should cause them to assist one another in the same way.

There are some verses on this subject, as follows:

"A citizen discoursing, not entirely in the Sanskrit language [18] nor wholly in the dialects of the country, on various topics in society, obtains great respect. The wise should not resort to a society disliked by the public, governed by no rules, and intent on the destruction of others. But a learned man living in a society which acts according to the wishes of the people and which has pleasure for its only object is highly respected in this world."

[18] This means, it is presumed, that the citizen should be acquainted with several languages. The middle part was perhaps a reference to the Thugs.

## Chapter V

### On the Kinds of Women Resorted to by the Citizen; and on Friends and Messengers

When Kama is practiced by men of the four classes, according to the rules of the Holy Writ (that is, by lawful marriage), with virgins of their own caste, it then becomes a means of acquiring lawful progeny and good fame, and it is not opposed to the customs of the world. On the contrary, the practice of Kama with women of the higher castes, and with those previously enjoyed by others, even though they be of the same caste, is prohibited. But the practice of Kama with women of the lower castes, with women excommunicated from their own caste, with public women, and with women twice married,[1] is neither enjoined nor prohibited. The object of practicing Kama with such women is pleasure only.

Nayikas,[2] therefore, are of three kinds, namely, maids, women twice married, and public women. Gonikaputra has

[1] This term does not apply to a widow, but to a woman who has probably left her husband, and is living with some other person as a married woman, *maritalement*, as they say in France.

[2] Any woman fit to be enjoyed without sin. The object of the enjoyment of women is twofold: pleasure and progeny. Any woman who can be enjoyed without sin for the purpose of accomplishing either the one or the other of these two objects is a Nayika. The fourth kind of Nayika which Vatsyayana admits further on is neither enjoyed for pleasure nor for progeny, but merely for accomplishing some special purpose in hand. The word Nayika is retained as a technical term throughout.

expressed an opinion that there is a fourth kind of Nayika: a woman who is resorted to on some special occasion even though she be previously married to another. These special occasions are when a man thinks thus:

This woman is self-willed, and has been previously enjoyed by many others besides myself. I may therefore safely resort to her as to a public woman though she belongs to a higher caste than mine, and in so doing I shall not be violating the ordinances of Dharma.

Or thus:
This is a twice-married woman and has been enjoyed by others before me; there is, therefore, no objection to my resorting to her.

Or thus:
This woman has gained the heart of her great and powerful husband, and exercises a mastery over him, who is a friend of my enemy; if, therefore, she becomes united with me she will cause her husband to abandon my enemy.

Or thus:
This woman will turn the mind of her husband, who is very powerful, in my favor, he being at present disaffected toward me, and intent on doing me some harm.

Or thus:
By making this woman my friend I shall gain the object of some friend of mine, or shall be able to effect the ruin of some enemy, or shall accomplish some other difficult purpose.

Or thus:
By being united with this woman, I shall kill her husband, and so obtain his vast riches which I covet.

Or thus:
The union of this woman with me is not attended with any

danger, and will bring me wealth, of which, on account of my poverty and inability to support myself, I am very much in need. I shall, therefore, obtain her vast riches in this way without any difficulty.

Or thus:
This woman loves me ardently, and knows all my weak points; if therefore I am unwilling to be united with her, she will make my faults public, and thus tarnish my character and reputation. Or she will bring some gross accusation against me, of which it may be hard to clear myself, and I shall be ruined. Or perhaps she will detach from me her husband, who is powerful and yet under her control, and will unite him to my enemy, or will herself join the latter.

Or thus:
The husband of this woman has violated the chastity of my wives; I shall therefore return that injury by seducing his wives.

Or thus:
By the help of this woman I shall kill an enemy of the king, who has taken shelter with her and whom I am ordered by the king to destroy.

Or thus:
The woman I love is under the control of this woman. I shall, through the influence of the latter, be able to get at the former.

Or thus:
This woman will bring to me a maid who possesses wealth and beauty but who is hard to get at, and under the control of another.

Or lastly thus:
My enemy is a friend of this woman's husband; I shall

therefore cause her to join him, and will thus create an enmity between her husband and him.

For these and similar reasons the wives of other men may be resorted to; but it must be distinctly understood that it is allowed only for special reasons, and not for mere carnal desire.

Charayana thinks that under these circumstances there is also a fifth kind of Nayika; namely, a woman who is kept by a minister, or who repairs to him occasionally; or a widow who accomplishes the purpose of a man with the person to whom she resorts.

Suvarnanabha adds that a woman who passes the life of an ascetic and in the condition of a widow may be considered as a sixth kind of Nayika.

Ghotakamukha cites the daughter of a public woman, and a female servant, who are still virgins, for a seventh kind of Nayika.

Gonardiya puts forth his doctrine that any woman born of good family, after she has come of age, is an eighth kind of Nayika.

But these last four kinds of Nayikas do not differ much from the first four kinds of them, as there is no separate object in resorting to them. Therefore, Vatsyayana is of opinion that there are only four kinds of Nayikas: the maid, the twice-married woman, the public woman, and the woman resorted to for a special purpose.

The following women are not to be enjoyed:

A leper
A lunatic
A woman turned out of caste
A woman who reveals secrets
A woman who publicly expresses a desire for sexual intercourse
A woman who is extremely white

A woman who is extremely black
A bad-smelling woman
A woman who is a near relative
A woman who is a female friend
A woman who leads the life of an ascetic
And, lastly, the wife of a relative, of a friend, of a learned Brahman, and of the king

The followers of Babhravya say that any woman who has been enjoyed by five men is a fit and proper person to be enjoyed. But Gonikaputra is of opinion that even when this is the case, the wives of a relative, of a learned Brahman, and of a king should be excepted.

The following are the kind of friends:

One who has played with you in the dust, that is, in childhood
One who is bound by an obligation
One who is of the same disposition and fond of the same things
One who is a fellow student
One who is acquainted with your secrets and faults, and whose faults and secrets are also known to you
One who is a child of your nurse
One who is brought up with you
One who is a hereditary friend

These friends should possess the following qualities:

They should tell the truth.
They should not be changed by time.
They should be favorable to your designs.
They should be firm.
They should be free from covetousness.
They should not be capable of being gained over by others.
They should not reveal your secrets.

Charayana says that citizens form friendships with washermen, barbers, cowherds, florists, druggists, betel-leaf sellers, tavern keepers, beggars, Pithamardas, Vitas, and Vidushakas, as also with the wives of all these people.

A messenger should possess the following qualities:

Skillfulness

Boldness

Knowledge of the intention of men by their outward signs

Absence of confusion, that is, no shyness

Knowledge of the exact meaning of what others do or say

Good manners

Knowledge of appropriate times and places for doing different things

Ingenuity in business

Quick comprehension

Quick application of remedies, that is, quick and ready resources

And this part ends with a verse:

"The man who is ingenious and wise, who is accompanied by a friend, and who knows the intentions of others, as well as the proper time and place for doing everything, can gain over, very easily, even a woman who is very hard to be obtained."

# PART TWO

*On Sexual Union*

———————

## Chapter 1

### Kinds of Union According to Dimensions, Force of Desire or Passion, and Time

Man is divided into three classes: the hare man, the bull man, and the horse man, according to the size of his lingam.

Woman also, according to the depth of her yoni is either a female deer, a mare, or a female elephant.

There are thus three equal unions between persons of corresponding dimensions, and there are six unequal unions when the dimensions do not correspond, or nine in all, as the following table shows:

| EQUAL | | UNEQUAL | |
| --- | --- | --- | --- |
| MEN | WOMEN | MEN | WOMEN |
| Hare | Deer | Hare | Mare |
| Bull | Mare | Hare | Elephant |
| Horse | Elephant | Bull | Deer |
| | | Bull | Elephant |
| | | Horse | Deer |
| | | Horse | Mare |

In these unequal unions, when the male exceeds the female in point of size, his union with a woman who is immediately next to him in size is called high union, and is of two kinds; while his union with the woman most remote from him in size is called the highest union, and is of one kind only. On the other hand, when the female exceeds the male in point of size, her union with a man immediately next to her in size is called low union, and is of two kinds; while her union with a man most remote from her in size is called the lowest union, and is of one kind only.

In other words, the horse and mare, the bull and deer, form the high union, while the horse and deer form the highest union. On the female side, the elephant and bull, the mare and hare, form low unions, while the elephant and the hare make the lowest unions.

There are, then, nine kinds of union according to dimensions. Among all these, equal unions are the best; those of a superlative degree, that is, the highest and the lowest, are the worst; and the rest are middling, and with them the high [1] are better than the low.

There are also nine kinds of union according to the force of passion or carnal desire, as follows:

| Men | Women | Men | Women |
|---|---|---|---|
| Small | Small | Small | Middling |
| Middling | Middling | Small | Intense |
| Intense | Intense | Middling | Small |
| | | Middling | Intense |
| | | Intense | Small |
| | | Intense | Middling |

A man is called a man of small passion whose desire at the time of sexual union is not great, whose semen is scanty, and who cannot bear the warm embraces of the female.

Those who differ from this temperament are called men of

[1] High unions are said to be better than low ones, for in the former it is possible for the male to satisfy his own passion without injuring the female, while in the latter it is difficult for the female to be satisfied by any means.

middling passion, while those of intense passion are full of desire.

In the same way, women are supposed to have the three degrees of feeling as specified above.

Lastly, according to time there are three kinds of men and women: the short-timed, the moderate-timed, and the long-timed, and of these, as in the previous statements, there are nine kinds of union.

But on this last head there is a difference of opinion about the female, which should be stated.

Auddalika says: "Females do not emit as males do. The males simply remove their desire, while the females, from their consciousness of desire, feel a certain kind of pleasure, which gives them satisfaction, but it is impossible for them to tell you what kind of pleasure they feel. The fact from which this becomes evident is that males, when engaged in coition, cease of themselves after emission, and are satisfied, but it is not so with females."

This opinion is, however, objected to on the grounds, that if a male be long-timed, the female loves him the more, but if he be short-timed she is dissatisfied with him. And this circumstance, some say, would prove that the female emits also.

But this opinion does not hold good, for if it takes a long time to allay a woman's desire, and during this time she is enjoying great pleasure, it is quite natural then that she should wish for its continuation. And on this subject there is a verse as follows:

"By union with men the lust, desire, or passion of women is satisfied, and the pleasure derived from the consciousness of it is called their satisfaction."

The followers of Babhravya, however, say that the semen of women continues to fall from the beginning of the sexual union to its end; and it is right that it should be so, for if they had no semen there would be no embryo.

To this there is an objection. In the beginning of coition

the passion of the woman is middling, and she cannot bear the vigorous thrusts of her lover; but by degrees her passion increases until she ceases to think about her body, and then finally she wishes to stop from further coition.

This objection, however, does not hold good, for even in ordinary things that revolve with great force, such as a potter's wheel or a top, we find that the motion at first is slow, but by degrees it becomes very rapid. In the same way the passion of the woman having gradually increased, she has a desire to discontinue coition, when all the semen has fallen away. And there is a verse with regard to this as follows:

"The fall of the semen of the man takes place only at the end of coition, while the semen of the woman falls continually; and after the semen of both has all fallen away then they wish for the discontinuance of coition."

Lastly, Vatsyayana is of opinion that the semen of the female falls in the same way as that of the male.

Now, someone may ask here: If men and women are beings of the same kind, and are engaged in bringing about the same result, why should they have different work to do?

Vatsyayana says that this is so because the ways of working, as well as the consciousness of pleasure in men and women, are different. The difference in the ways of working, by which men are the actors and women are the persons acted upon, is owing to the nature of the male and the female; otherwise the actor would be sometimes the person acted upon, and vice versa. And from this difference in the ways of working follows the difference in the consciousness of pleasure, for a man thinks, "This woman is united with me," and a woman thinks, "I am united with this man."

It may be said that if the ways of working in men and women are different, why should there not be a difference, even in the pleasure they feel, which is the result of those ways?

But this objection is groundless, for the person acting and the person acted upon being of different kinds, there is a reason for the difference in their ways of working; but there is no reason for any difference in the pleasure they feel, because they both naturally derive pleasure from the act they perform.[2]

On this again some may say that when different persons are engaged in doing the same work, we find that they accomplish the same end or purpose; while, on the contrary, in the case of men and women we find that each of them accomplishes his or her own end separately, and this is inconsistent. But this is a mistake, for we find that sometimes two things are done at the same time; as for instance in the fighting of rams, both the rams receive the shock at the same time on their heads. Or in throwing one wood apple against another, or in a fight or struggle of wrestlers. If it be said that in these cases the things employed are of the same kind, it is answered that even in the case of men and women, the nature of the two persons is the same. And as the difference in their ways of working arises from the difference of their conformation only, it follows that men experience the same kind of pleasure as women do. There is also a verse on this subject as follows:

"Men and women being of the same nature feel the same kind of pleasure, and therefore a man should marry such a woman as will love him ever afterward."

The pleasure of men and women being thus proved to be of the same kind, it follows that in regard to time there are

[2] This is a long dissertation very common among Sanskrit authors, both when writing and talking socially. They start certain propositions, and then argue for and against them. What it is presumed the author means is that, though both men and women derive pleasure from the act of coition, the way it is produced is brought about by different means, each individual performing his own work in the matter irrespective of the other, and each deriving individually his own consciousness of pleasure from the act performed. There is a difference in the work that each does, and a difference in the consciousness of pleasure that each has, but no difference in the pleasure they feel, for each feels that pleasure to a greater or lesser degree.

nine kinds of sexual intercourse, in the same way as there are nine kinds according to the force of passion.

There being thus nine kinds of union with regard to dimensions, force of passion, and time, respectively, by making combinations of them innumerable kinds of union would be produced. Therefore in each particular kind of sexual union, men should use such means as they may think suitable for the occasion.

At the first time of sexual union the passion of the male is intense, and his time is short, but in subsequent unions on the same day the reverse of this is the case. With the female, however, it is the contrary, for at the first time her passion is weak, and her time long, but on subsequent occasions on the same day her passion is intense and her time short, until her passion is satisfied.

## On the Different Kinds of Love

Men learned in the humanities are of opinion that love is of four kinds:

1. Love acquired by continual habit
2. Love resulting from the imagination
3. Love resulting from belief
4. Love resulting from the perception of external objects

(1). Love resulting from the constant and continual performance of some act is called love acquired by constant practice and habit; as for instance, the love of sexual intercourse, the love of hunting, the love of drinking, the love of gambling, and so on.

(2). Love which is felt for things to which we are not habituated, and which proceeds entirely from ideas, is called love resulting from imagination; as for instance, that love which some men and women and eunuchs feel for the Auparishtaka, or mouth congress, and that which is felt by all for such things as embracing, kissing, and so on.

(3). The love which is mutual on both sides, and proved to be true, when each looks upon the other as his or her very own; such is called love resulting from belief by the learned.

(4). The love resulting from the perception of external objects is quite evident and well known to the world, because the pleasure it affords is superior to the pleasure of the other kinds of love, which exist only for its sake.

What has been said in this chapter upon the subject of sexual union is sufficient for the learned; but for the edification of the ignorant, the same will now be treated at length and in detail.

## Chapter II

### On the Embrace

This part of the *Kama Shastra,* which treats of sexual union, is also called "Sixty-four" (Chatushshashti). Some old authors say that it is called so because it contains sixty-four chapters. Others are of opinion that the author of this part being a person named Panchala, and the person who recited the part of the Rig-Veda called "Dashatapa," which contains sixty-four verses, being also called Panchala, the name "Sixty-four" has been given to the part of the work in honor of the Rig-Veda. The followers of Badhravya say on the other hand that this part contains eight subjects: the embrace, kissing, scratching with the nails or fingers, biting, lying down, making various sounds, playing the part of a man, and the Auparishataka, or mouth congress. Each of these subjects being of eight kinds, and eight multiplied by eight being sixty-four, this part is therefore named "Sixty-four." But Vatsyayana affirms that as this part contains also the following subjects, namely striking, crying, the acts of a man during congress, the various kinds of congress, and other subjects, the name "Sixty-four" is given to it only accidentally. As for instance, we say this tree is "Saptaparna," or seven-leaved; this offering of rice is "Pancha-varna," or five-colored; but the tree has not seven leaves, nor has the rice five colors.

However, the part "Sixty-four" is now treated of; and the embrace, being the first subject, will now be considered.

The embrace which indicates the mutual love of a man and woman who have come together is of four kinds:

> Touching
> Piercing
> Rubbing
> Pressing

The action in each case is denoted by the meaning of the word which stands for it.

(1). When a man under some pretext or other goes in front of or alongside a woman and touches her body with his own, it is called the "touching embrace."

(2) When a woman in a lonely place bends down, as if to pick up something, and pierces, as it were, a man sitting or standing, with her breasts, and the man in return takes hold of them, it is called a "piercing embrace."

These two embraces take place only between persons who do not, as yet, speak freely with each other.

(3). When two lovers are walking slowly together, either in the dark or in a place of public resort, or in a lonely place, and rub their bodies against each other, it is called a "rubbing embrace."

(4). When on the above occasion one of them presses the other's body forcibly against a wall or pillar, it is called a "pressing embrace."

These two last embraces are peculiar to those who know the intentions of each other.

At the times of meeting, the four following kinds of embrace are used:

*Jataveshtitaka,* or the twining of a creeper.
*Vriskshadhirudhaka,* or climbing a tree.
*Tila-Tandulaka,* or the mixture of sesame seed with rice.
*Kshiraniraka,* or milk-and-water embrace.

(1). When a woman, clinging to a man as a creeper twines round a tree, bends his head down to hers with the desire of kissing him and slightly makes the sound of *Sūt, sūt*, embraces him, and looks lovingly toward him, it is called an embrace like the "twining of a creeper."

(2). When a woman, having placed one of her feet on the foot of her lover, and the other on one of his thighs, passes one of her arms round his back, and the other on his shoulders, makes slightly the sounds of singing and cooing, and wishes, as it were, to climb up him in order to have a kiss, it is called an embrace like the "climbing of a tree."

These two embraces take place when the lover is standing.

(3). When lovers lie on a bed, and embrace each other so closely that the arms and thighs of one are encircled by the arms and thighs of the other, and are, as it were rubbing up against them, this is called an embrace like "the mixture of sesame seed with rice."

(4). When a man and a woman are very much in love with each other, and, not thinking of any pain or hurt, embrace each other as if they were entering into each other's bodies either while the woman is sitting on the lap of the man or in front of him, or on a bed, then it is called an embrace like a "mixture of milk and water."

These two embraces take place at the time of sexual union.

Babhravya has thus related to us the above eight kinds of embraces.

Suvarnanabha, moreover, gives us four ways of embracing simple members of the body, which are:

The embrace of the thighs
The embrace of the *jaghana*, that is, the part of the body from the navel downward to the thighs
The embrace of the breasts
The embrace of the forehead

(1). When one of two lovers presses forcibly one or both

of the thighs of the other between his or her own, it is called the "embrace of thighs."

(2). When the man presses the jaghana, or middle part, of the woman's body against his own, and mounts upon her to practice, either scratching with the nail or finger, or biting or striking or kissing, the hair of the woman being loose and flowing, it is called the "embrace of the jaghana."

(3). When a man places his breast between the breasts of a woman and presses her with it, it is called the "embrace of the breasts."

(4). When either of the lovers touches the mouth, the eyes, and the forehead of the other with his or her own, it is called the "embrace of the forehead."

Some say that even shampooing is a kind of embrace, because there is a touching of bodies in it. But Vatsyayana thinks that shampooing is performed at a different time, and for a different purpose; and as it is also of a different character, it cannot be said to be included in the embrace. There are also some verses on the subject, as follows:

"The whole subject of embracing is of such nature that men who ask questions about it, or who hear about it, or who talk about it, acquire thereby a desire for enjoyment. Even those embraces that are not mentioned in the *Kama Shastra* should be practiced at the time of sexual enjoyment, if they are in any way conducive to the increase of love or passion. The rules of the Shastra apply as long as the passion of man is middling, but when the wheel of love is once set in motion, there is then no Shastra and no order."

## Chapter III

### On Kissing

It is said by some that there is no fixed time or order between the embrace, the kiss, and the pressing or scratching with the nails or fingers, but that all these things should be done generally before sexual union takes place, while striking and making the various sounds generally takes place at the time of the union. Vatsyayana, however, thinks that anything may take place at any time, for love does not care for time or order.

On the occasion of first congress, kissing and the other things mentioned above should be done moderately; they should not be continued for a long time, and should be done alternately. On subsequent occasions, however, the reverse of all this may take place, and moderation will not be necessary; they may continue for a long time; and for the purpose of kindling love, they may be all done at the same time.

The following are the places for kissing: the forehead, the eyes, the cheeks, the throat, the bosom, the breasts, the lips, and the interior of the mouth. Moreover, the people of the Lat country kiss also the following places: the joints of the thighs, the arms, and the navel. But Vatsyayana thinks that though kissing is practiced by these people in the above places because of the intensity of their love and the customs of their country, it is not fit to be practiced by all.

Now, with a young girl there are three sorts of kisses:

The nominal kiss
The throbbing kiss
The touching kiss

(1). When a girl touches only the mouth of her lover with her own, but does not herself do anything, it is called the "nominal kiss."

(2). When a girl, setting aside her bashfulness a little, wishes to touch the lip that is pressed into her mouth, and with that object moves her lower lip, but not the upper one, it is called the "throbbing kiss."

(3). When a girl touches her lover's lip with her tongue, and having shut her eyes, places her hands on those of her lover, it is called the "touching kiss."

Other authors describe four other kinds of kisses:

The straight kiss
The bent kiss
The turned kiss
The pressed kiss

(1). When the lips of two lovers are brought into direct contact with each other, it is called a "straight kiss."

(2). When the heads of two lovers are bent toward each other, and when so bent, kissing takes place, it is called a "bent kiss."

(3). When one of them turns up the face of the other by holding the head and chin, and then kissing, it is called a "turned kiss."

(4). Lastly, when the lower lip is pressed with much force, it is called a "pressed kiss."

There is also a fifth kind of kiss, called the "greatly pressed kiss," which is effected by taking hold of the lower lip between two fingers, and then after touching it with the tongue, pressing it with great force with the lip.

As regards kissing, a wager may be laid as to which will

get hold of the lips of the other first. If the woman loses, she should pretend to cry, should keep her lover off by shaking her hands, and turn away from him and dispute with him, saying, "Let another wager be laid." If she loses this a second time, she should appear doubly distressed, and when her lover is off his guard or asleep, she should get hold of his lower lip, and hold it in her teeth, so that it should not slip away; and then she should laugh, make a loud noise, deride him, dance about, and say whatever she likes in a joking way, moving her eyebrows, and rolling her eyes. Such are the wagers and quarrels as far as kissing is concerned, but the same may be applied with regard to the pressing or scratching with the nails and fingers, biting and striking. All these, however, are peculiar only to men and women of intense passion.

When a man kisses the upper lip of a woman, while she in return kisses his lower lip, it is called the "kiss of the upper lip."

When one of them takes both the lips of the other between his or her own, it is called "a clasping kiss." A woman, however, takes this kind of kiss only from a man who has no moustache. And on the occasion of this kiss, if one of them touches the teeth, the tongue, and the palate of the other, with his or her tongue, it is called the "fighting of the tongue." In the same way, the pressing of the teeth of the one against the mouth of the other is to be practiced.

Kissing is of four kinds: moderate, contracted, pressed, and soft, according to the different parts of the body which are kissed, for different kinds of kisses are appropriate for different parts of the body.

When a woman looks at the face of her lover while he is asleep, and kisses it to show her intention or desire, it is called a "kiss that kindles love."

When a woman kisses her lover while he is engaged in business, or while he is quarreling with her, or while he is looking at something else, so that his mind may be turned away, it is called a "kiss that turns away."

When a lover coming home late at night kisses his beloved who is asleep on her bed, in order to show her his desire, it is called a "kiss that awakens." On such an occasion the woman may pretend to be asleep at the time of her lover's arrival, so that she may know his intention and obtain respect from him.

When a person kisses the reflection of the person he loves in a mirror, in water, or on a wall, it is called a "kiss showing the intention."

When a person kisses a child sitting on his lap, or a picture or an image or figure, in the presence of the person beloved by him, it is called a "transferred kiss."

When at night at a theater, or in an assembly of caste men, a man coming up to a woman kisses a finger of her hand if she be standing, or a toe of her foot if she be sitting, or when a woman in shampooing her lover's body places her face in his thigh (as if she were sleepy) so as to inflame his passion, and kisses his thigh or great toe, it is called a "demonstrative kiss."

There is also a verse on this subject as follows:

"Whatever things may be done by one of the lovers to the other, the same should be returned by the other; that is, if the woman kisses him he should kiss her in return; if she strikes him he should also strike her in return."

## Chapter IV

### On Pressing or Marking or Scratching With the Nails

When love becomes intense, pressing with the nails or scratching the body with them is practiced, and it is done on the following occasions: on the first visit; at the time of setting out on a journey; on the return from a journey; at the time when an angry lover is reconciled; and, lastly, when the woman is intoxicated.

But pressing with the nails is not a usual thing except with those who are intensely passionate. It is employed, together with biting, by those to whom the practice is agreeable.

Pressing with the nails is of the eight following kinds, according to the forms of the marks which are produced:

1. Sounding
2. Half-moon
3. A circle
4. A line
5. A tiger's nail or claw
6. A peacock's foot
7. The jump of a hare
8. The leaf of a blue lotus

The places that are to be pressed with the nails are: the armpit, the throat, the breasts, the lips, the jaghana, or middle parts of the body, and the thighs. But Suvarnanabha is of the opinion that when the impetuosity of passion is excessive, then the places need not be considered.

The qualities of good nails are that they should be bright, well set, clean, entire, convex, soft, and glossy in appearance. Nails are of three kinds according to their size:

> Small
> Middling
> Large

Large nails, which give grace to the hands, and attract the hearts of women from their appearance, are possessed by the Bengalese.

Small nails, which can be used in various ways, and are to be applied only with the object of giving pleasure, are possessed by the people of the southern districts.

Middling nails, which contain the properties of both the above kinds, belong to the people of Maharashtra.

(1). When a person presses the chin, the breasts, the lower lip, or the jaghana of another so softly that no scratch or mark is left, but only the hair on the body becomes erect from the touch of the nails, and the nails themselves make a sound, it is called a "sounding or pressing with the nails."

This pressing is used in the case of a young girl when her lover shampoos her, scratches her head, and wants to trouble or frighten her.

(2). The curved mark with the nails, which is impressed on the neck and the breasts, is called the "half-moon."

(3). When the half-moons are impressed opposite each other, it is called a "circle." This mark with the nails is generally made on the navel, the small cavities about the buttocks, and on the joints of the thigh.

(4). A mark in the form of a small line, which can be made on any part of the body, is called a "line."

(5). This same line, when it is curved, and made on the breast, is called a "tiger's nail."

(6). When a curved mark is made on the breast by means of the five nails, it is called a "peacock's foot." This mark is made with the object of being praised, for it requires a great deal of skill to make it properly.

(7). When five marks with the nails are made close to one another near the nipple of the breast, it is called "the jump of a hare."

(8). A mark made on the breast or on the hips in the form of a leaf of the blue lotus is called the "leaf of a blue lotus."

When a person is going on a journey, and makes a mark on the thighs, or on the breast, it is called a "token of remembrance." On such an occasion three or four lines are impressed close to one another with the nails.

Here ends discourse of the marking with the nails. Marks of kinds other than the above may also be made with the nails, for the ancient authors say that as there are innumerable degrees of skill among men (the practice of this art being known to all), so there are innumerable ways of making these marks. And as pressing or marking with the nails is dependent on love, no one can say with certainty how many different kinds of marks with the nails do actually exist. The reason for this is, Vatsyayana says, that as variety is necessary in love, so love is to be produced by means of variety. It is on this account that courtesans, who are well acquainted with various ways and means, become so desirable; for if variety is sought in all the arts and amusements, such as archery and others, how much more should it be sought after in the art of love.

The marks of the nails should not be made on married women, but particular kinds of marks may be made on their private parts for the remembrance and increase of love.

There are also some verses on the subject, as follows:

"The love of a woman who sees the marks of nails on the private parts of her body, even though they are old and almost worn out, becomes again fresh and new. If there be no marks of nails to remind a person of the passages of love, then love is lessened in the same way as when no union takes place for a long time."

Even when a stranger sees at a distance a young woman with the marks of nails on her breast,[1] he is filled with love and respect for her.

A man, also, who carries the marks of nails and teeth on some parts of his body, influences the mind of a woman, even though it be ever so firm. In short, nothing tends to increase love so much as the effects of marking with the nails, and biting.

[1] From this it would appear that in ancient times the breasts of women were not covered, and this is seen in the painting of the Ajanta and other caves, where we find that the breasts of even royal ladies and others are exposed.

## Chapter V

*On Biting, and the Means to Be Employed With
Regard to Women of Different Countries*

All the places that can be kissed are also the places that can
be bitten, except the upper lip, the interior of the mouth,
and the eyes.

The qualities of good teeth are as follows: They should be
equal, possessed of a pleasing brightness, capable of being
colored, of proper proportions, unbroken, and with sharp
ends.

The defects of teeth, on the other hand, are that they are
blunt, protruding from the gums, rough, soft, large, and
loosely set.

The following are the different kinds of biting:

> The hidden bite
> The swollen bite
> The point
> The line of points
> The coral and the jewel
> The line of jewels
> The broken cloud
> The biting of the boar

(1). The biting which is shown only by the excessive
redness of the skin that is bitten, is called the "hidden bite."

(2). When the skin is pressed down on both sides, it is
called the "swollen bite."

(3). When a small portion of the skin is bitten with two teeth only, it is called the "point."

(4). When such small portions of the skin are bitten with all the teeth, it is called the "line of points."

(5). The biting which is done by bringing together the teeth and the lips is called the "coral and the jewel." The lips are the coral, and the teeth are the jewel.

(6). When biting is done with all the teeth, it is called the "line of jewels."

(7). The biting which consists of unequal risings in a circle, and which comes from the space between the teeth, is called the "broken cloud." This is impressed on the breasts.

(8). The biting which consists of many broad rows of marks near to one another, and with red intervals, is called the "biting of a boar." This is impressed on the breasts and the shoulders; and these two last modes of biting are peculiar to persons of intense passion.

The lower lip is the place on which the "hidden bite," the "swollen bite," and the "point" are made; the "swollen bite" and the "coral and the jewel" bite are done on the cheek. Kissing, pressing with the nails, and biting are the ornaments of the left cheek, and when the word "cheek" is used, it is to be understood as the left cheek.

Both the "line of points" and the "line of jewels" are to be impressed on the throat, the armpit, and the joints of the thighs; but the "line of points" alone is to be impressed on the forehead and the thighs.

The marking with the nails, and the biting of the following things, namely, an ornament of the forehead, an ear ornament, a bunch of flowers, a betel leaf, or a tamala leaf, which are worn by or belong to the woman who is beloved, are signs of desire of enjoyment.

Here ends discourse of the different kinds of biting.

In the affairs of love a man should do such things as are agreeable to the women of different countries.

The women of the central countries (that is, between the

Ganges and the Jumna) are noble in their character, not accustomed to disgraceful practices, and dislike pressing with the nails and biting.

The women of the Balhika country are gained over by striking.

The women of Avantika are fond of foul pleasures, and have not good manners.

The women of Maharashtra are fond of practicing the sixty-four arts; they utter low and harsh words, and like to be spoken to in the same way, and have an impetuous desire of enjoyment.

The women of Pataliputra (that is, the modern Patna) are of the same nature as the women of the Maharashtra, but show their likings only in secret.

The women of the Dravidian country, though they are rubbed and pressed about at the time of sexual enjoyment, have a slow fall of semen: that is, they are very slow in the act of coition.

The women of Vanavasi are moderately passionate; they go through every kind of enjoyment, cover their bodies, and abuse those who utter low, mean, and harsh words.

The women of Avanti hate kissing, marking with the nails, and biting, but they have a fondness for various kinds of sexual union.

The women of Malwa like embracing and kissing, but not wounding, and they are gained over by striking.

The women of Abhira, and those of the country about the Indus and five rivers (that is, the Punjab), are gained over by the Auparishtaka, or mouth congress.

The women of Aparatika are full of passion, and make slowly the sound *Sit*.

The women of the Lat country have even more impetuous desire, and also make the sound *Sit*.

The women of the Stri Rajya and of Koshala (Oudh) are full of impetuous desire; their semen falls in large quantities, and they are fond of taking medicine to make it do so.

The women of the Andhra country have tender bodies; they are fond of enjoyment, and have a liking for voluptuous pleasures.

The women of Gandak have tender bodies, and speak sweetly.

Now, Suvarnanabha is of opinion that that which is agreeable to the nature of a particular person is of more consequence than that which is agreeable to a whole nation, and that therefore the peculiarities of the country should not be observed in such cases. The various pleasures, the dress, and the sports of one country are in time borrowed by another, and in such a case these things must be considered as belonging originally to that country.

Among the things mentioned above, namely, embracing, kissing, and so on, those which increase passion should be done first, and those which are only for amusement or variety should be done afterward.

There are also some verses on this subject, as follows:

"When a man bites a woman forcibly, she should angrily do the same to him with double force. Thus a 'point' should be returned with a 'line of points,' and a 'line of points' with a 'broken cloud'; and if she be excessively chaffed, she should at once begin a love quarrel with him. At such a time she should take hold of her lover by the hair, and bend his head down, and kiss his lower lip, and then, being intoxicated with love, she should shut her eyes and bite him in various places. Even by day and in a place of public resort, when her lover shows her any mark that she may have inflicted on his body, she should smile at the sight of it, and turning her face as if she were going to chide him, she should show him with an angry look the marks on her own body that have been made by him. Thus if men and women act according to each other's liking, their love for each other will not be lessened even in one hundred years."

## Chapter VI

### On the Various Ways of Lying Down, and the Different Kinds of Congress

On the occasion of a "high congress" the Mrigi (Deer) woman should lie down in such a way as to widen her yoni, while in a "low congress" the Hastini (Elephant) woman should lie down so as to contract hers. But in an "equal congress" they should lie down in the natural position. What is said above concerning the Mrigi and the Hastini applies also to the Vadawa (Mare) woman. In a "low congress" the woman should particularly make use of medicine, to cause her desires to be satisfied quickly.

The Deer woman has the following three ways of lying down:

> The widely opened position
> The yawning position
> The position of the wife of Indra

(1). When she lowers her head and raises her middle parts, it is called the "widely opened position." At such a time the man should apply some unguent, so as to make the entrance easy.

(2). When she raises her thighs and keeps them wide apart and engages in congress, it is called the "yawning position."

(3). When she places her thighs with her legs doubled

on them upon her sides, and thus engages in congress, it is called the position of Indrani, and this is learned only by practice. The position is also useful in the case of the "highest congress."

There are also the "clasping position" and the "low congress," and in the "lowest congress," together with the "pressing position," the "twining position" and the "mare's position."

When the legs of both the male and the female are stretched straight out over each other, it is called the "clasping position." It is of two kinds, the side position and the supine position, according to the way in which they lie down. In the side position the male should invariably lie on his left side, and cause the woman to lie on her right side, and this rule is to be observed in lying down with all kinds of women.

When, after congress has begun in the clasping position, the woman presses her lover with her thighs, it is called the "pressing position."

When the woman places one of her thighs across the thigh of her lover, it is called the "twining position."

When the woman forcibly holds in her yoni the lingam after it is in, it is called the "mare's position." This is learned by practice only, and is chiefly found among the women of the Andra country.

The above are the different ways of lying down, mentioned by Babhravya; Suvarnanabha, however, gives the following in addition:

When the female raises both of her thighs straight up, it is called the "rising position."

When she raises both of her legs, and places them on her lover's shoulders, it is called the "yawning position."

When the legs are contracted, and thus held by the lover before his bosom, it is called the "pressed position."

When only one of her legs is stretched out, it is called the "half-pressed position."

When the woman places one of her legs on her lover's

shoulder, and stretches the other out, and then places the latter on his shoulder, and stretches out the other, and continues to do so alternately, it is called the "splitting of a bamboo."

When one of her legs is placed on the head, and the other is stretched out, it is called the "fixing of a nail." This is learned by practice only.

When both the legs of the woman are contracted, and placed on her stomach, it is called the "crab's position."

When the thighs are raised and placed one upon the other, it is called the "packed position."

When the shanks are placed one upon the other, it is called the "lotus-like position."

When a man, during congress, turns round, and enjoys the woman without leaving her, while she embraces him round the back all the time, it is called the "turning position," and is learned only by practice.

Thus, says Suvarnanabha, these different ways of lying down, sitting, and standing should be practiced in water, because it is easy to do so therein. But Vatsyayana is of opinion that congress in water is improper, because it is prohibited by the religious law.

When a man and a woman support themselves on each other's bodies, or on a wall or pillar, and thus while standing engage in congress, it is called the "supported congress."

When a man supports himself against a wall, and the woman, sitting on his hands joined together and held underneath her, throws her arms round his neck, and putting her thighs alongside his waist, moves herself by her feet, which are touching the wall against which the man is leaning, it is called the "suspended congress."

When a woman stands on her hands and feet like a quadruped, and her lover mounts her like a bull, it is called the "congress of a cow." At this time everything that is ordinarily done on the bosom should be done on the back.

In the same way can be carried on the congress of a dog,

the congress of a goat, the congress of a deer, the forcible mounting of an ass, the congress of a cat, the jump of a tiger, the pressing of an elephant, the rubbing of a boar, and the mounting of a horse. And in all these cases the characteristics of the different animals should be manifested by acting like them.

When a man enjoys two women at the same time, both of whom love him equally, it is called the "united congress."

When a man enjoys many women altogether, it is called the "congress of a herd of cows."

The following kinds of congress, namely, sporting in water, or the congress of an elephant with many female elephants which is said to take place only in the water, the congress of a collection of goats, the congress of a collection of deer, take place in imitation of these animals.

In Gramaneri many young men enjoy a woman that may be married to one of them, either one after the other or at the same time. Thus one of them holds her, another enjoys her, a third uses her mouth, a fourth holds her middle part, and in this way they go on enjoying her several parts alternately.

The same things can be done when several men are sitting in company with one courtesan, or when one courtesan is alone with many men. In the same way this can be done by the women of the king's harem when they accidentally get hold of a man.

The people in the Southern countries have also a congress in the anus, that is called the "lower congress."

Thus ends the various kinds of congress. There are also two verses on the subjects, as follows:

"An ingenious person should multiply the kinds of congress after the fashion of the different kinds of beasts and of birds. For these different kinds of congress, performed according to the usage of each country, and the liking of each individual, generate love, friendship, and respect in the hearts of women."

## Chapter VII

### On the Various Modes of Striking, and on the Sounds Appropriate to Them

Sexual intercourse can be compared to a quarrel, on account of the contrarieties of love and its tendency to dispute. The place of striking with passion is the body, and on the body the special places are:

> The shoulders
> The head
> The space between the breasts
> The back
> The jaghana, or middle part of the body
> The sides

Striking is of four kinds:

> Striking with the back of the hand
> Striking with the fingers a little contracted
> Striking with the fist
> Striking with the open palm of the hand.

On account of its causing pain, striking gives rise to the kissing sound, which is of various kinds, and to the eight kinds of crying:

> The sound *Hin*
> The thundering sound

The cooing sound
The weeping sound
The sound *Phut*
The sound *Phât*
The sound *Sût*
The sound *Plât*

Besides these, there are also words having a meaning, such as "mother," and those that are expressive of prohibition, sufficiency, desire of liberation, pain or praise, and to which may be added sounds like those of the dove, the cuckoo, the green pigeon, the parrot, the bee, the sparrow, the flamingo, the duck, and the quail, which are all occasionally made use of.

Blows with the fist should be given on the back of the woman, while she is sitting on the lap of the man, and she should give blows in return, abusing the man as if she were angry, and making the cooing and the weeping sounds. While the woman is engaged in congress the space between the breasts should be struck with the back of the hand, slowly at first, and then proportionately to the increasing excitement, until the end.

At this time the sounds *Hin* and others may be made, alternately or optionally, according to habit. When the man, making the sound *Phât,* strikes the woman on the head with the fingers of his hand a little contracted, it is called Pras-ritaka, which means striking with the fingers of the hand a little contracted. In this case the appropriate sounds are the cooing sound, the sound *Phât,* and the sound *Phut* in the interior of the mouth, and at the end of congress the sighing and weeping sounds. The sound *Phât* is an imitation of the sound of a bamboo being split, while the sound *Phut* is like the sound made by something falling into water. At all times when kissing and suchlike things are begun, the woman should give a reply with a kissing sound. During the excitement, when the woman is not accustomed to striking, she continually utters words expressive of prohibition, sufficiency, or desire of liberation, as well as the words "father," "mother," intermingled with the sighing, weeping, and thundering sound. Toward the conclusion of the congress, the breasts, the jaghana, and the sides of the women should be pressed with the open palms of the hand, with some force, until the end of it, and then sounds like those of the quail or the goose should be made.

There are also two verses on the subject, as follows:

"The characteristics of manhood are said to consist of roughness and impetuosity, while weakness, tenderness, sensibility, and an inclination to turn away from unpleasant things are the distinguishing marks of womanhood. The excitement of passion, and peculiarities of habit, may sometimes cause contrary results to appear, but these do not last long, and in the end the natural state is resumed."

The wedge on the bosom, the scissors on the head, the piercing instrument on the cheeks, and the pincers on the breasts and sides may also be taken into consideration with the other four modes of striking, and thus give eight ways altogether. But these four ways of striking with instruments are peculiar to the people of the southern countries, and the marks caused by them are seen on the breasts of their women. They are local peculiarities, but Vatsyayana is of the opinion that the practice of them is painful, barbarous, and base, and quite unworthy of imitation.

In the same way anything that is a local peculiarity should not always be adopted elsewhere, and even in the place where the practice is prevalent, excess of it should always be avoided. Instances of the dangerous use of them may be given as follows. The King of the Panchalas killed the courtesan Madhavasena by means of the wedge during congress. King Satakarni Satavahana of the Kuntala, deprived his great Queen Malayavati of her life by a pair of scissors, and Naradeva, whose hand was deformed, blinded a dancing girl by directing a piercing instrument in a wrong way.

There are also two verses on the subject, as follows:

"About these things there cannot be either enumeration or any definite rule. Congress having once commenced, passion alone gives birth to all the acts of the parties."

Such passionate actions and amorous gesticulations or movements, which arise on the spur of the moment, and during sexual intercourse, cannot be defined, and are as irregular as dreams. A horse having once attained the fifth degree of motion goes on with blind speed, regardless of pits, ditches, and posts in his way; and in the same manner a loving pair become blind with passion in the heat of congress, and go on with great impetuosity, paying not the least regard to excess. For this reason one who is well acquainted with the science of love, and knowing his own strength as also the tenderness, impetuosity, and strength of the young woman, should act accordingly. The various modes of enjoyment are not for all times or for all persons, but should be used only at the proper time, and in the proper countries and places.

## Chapter VIII

### On Women Acting the Part of a Man; and on the Work of a Man

When a woman sees that her lover is fatigued by constant congress, without having his desire satisfied, she should, with his permission, lay him down upon his back, and give him assistance by acting his part. She may also do this to satisfy the curiosity of her lover, or her own desire of novelty.

There are two ways of doing this: the first is when during congress she turns round, and gets on top of her lover, in such a manner as to continue the congress, without obstructing the pleasure of it; and the other is when she acts the man's part from the beginning. At such a time, with flowers in her hair hanging loose, and her smiles broken by hard breathings, she should press upon her lover's bosom with her own breasts; and, lowering her head frequently, she should do in return the same actions which he used to do before, returning his blows and chaffing him. She should say, "I was laid down by you, and fatigued with hard congress; I shall now therefore lay you down in return." She should then again manifest her own bashfulness, her fatigue, and her desire of stopping the congress. In this way she should do the work of a man, which we shall presently relate.

Whatever is done by a man for giving pleasure to a woman is called the work of a man, and is as follows:

While the woman is lying on his bed, and is as it were abstracted by his conversation, he should loosen the knot of her undergarments, and when she begins to dispute with him he should overwhelm her with kisses. Then when his lingam is erect he should touch her with his hands in various places, and gently manipulate various parts of the body. If the woman is bashful, and if it is the first time that they have come together, the man should place his hands between her thighs, which she would probably keep close together; and if she is a very young girl, he should first get his hands upon her breasts, which she would probably cover with her own hands, and under her armpits and on her neck. If, however, she is a seasoned woman, he should do whatever is agreeable either to him or to her, and whatever is fitting for the occasion. After this, he should take hold of her hair, and hold her chin in his fingers for the purpose of kissing her. On this, if she is a young girl, she will become bashful and close her eyes. In any event, he should gather from the action of the woman what things would be pleasing to her during congress.

Here Suvarnanabha says that while a man is doing to the woman what he likes best during congress, he should always make a point of pressing those parts of her body on which she turns her eyes.

The signs of the enjoyment and satisfaction of the woman are as follows: her body relaxes, she closes her eyes, she puts aside all bashfulness, and shows increased willingness to unite the two organs as closely together as possible. On the other hand, the signs of her want of enjoyment and of failing to be satisfied are as follows: she shakes her hands, she does not let the man get up, feels dejected, bites the man, kicks him, and continues to go on moving after the man has finished. In such cases the man should rub the yoni of the woman with his hand and fingers (as the elephant rubs anything with his trunk) before engaging in congress, until it is softened, and after that is done he should proceed to put his lingam into her.

The acts to be done by the man are:

Moving forward
Friction or churning
Piercing
Rubbing
Pressing
Giving a blow
The blow of a boar
The blow of a bull
The sporting of a sparrow

(1). When the organs are brought together properly and directly, it is called "moving the organ forward."

(2). When the lingam is held with the hand, and turned all round in the yoni, it is called a "churning."

(3). When the yoni is lowered, and the upper part of it is struck with the lingam, it is called "piercing."

(4). When the same thing is done on the lower part of the yoni, it is called "rubbing."

(5). When the yoni is pressed by the lingam for a long time, it is called "pressing."

(6). When the lingam is removed to some distance from the yoni, and then forcibly strikes it, it is called "giving a blow."

(7). When only one part of the yoni is rubbed with the lingam, it is called the "blow of a boar."

(8). When both sides of the yoni are rubbed in this way, it is called the "blow of a bull."

(9). When the lingam is in the yoni, and is moved up and down frequently, and without being taken out, it is called the "sporting of a sparrow." This takes place at the end of congress.

When a woman acts the part of a man, she has the following things to do in addition to the nine given above:

The pair of tongs
The top
The swing

(1). When the woman holds the lingam in her yoni, draws it in, presses it, and keeps it thus in her for a long time, it is called the "pair of tongs."

(2). When, while engaged in congress, she turns round like a wheel, it is called the "top." This is learned by practice only.

(3). When, on such an occasion, the man lifts up the middle part of his body, and the woman turns round her middle part, it is called the "swing."

When the woman is tired, she should place her forehead on that of her lover, and should thus take rest without disturbing the union of the organs; and when the woman has rested herself the man should turn round and begin the congress again.

There are also some verses on the subject, as follows:

"Though a woman is reserved, and keeps her feelings concealed, yet when she gets on top a man, she then shows all her love and desire. A man should gather from the actions of the woman of what disposition she is, and in what way she likes to be enjoyed. A woman during her monthly courses, a woman who has been lately confined, and a fat woman should not be made to act the part of a man."

## Chapter IX

### On the Auparishtaka,[1] or Mouth Congress

There are two kinds of eunuchs, those that are disguised as males and those that are disguised as females. Eunuchs disguised as females imitate their dress, speech, gestures, tenderness, timidity, simplicity, softness, and bashfulness. The acts that are done on the jaghana, or middle parts, of women, are done in the mouths of these eunuchs, and this is called Auparishtaka. These eunuchs derive their imaginative pleasure, and their livelihood, from this kind of congress, and they lead the life of courtesans. So much concerning eunuchs disguised as females.

Eunuchs disguised as males keep their desires secret, and when they wish to do anything they lead the life of shampooers. Under the pretense of shampooing, a eunuch of this

[1] This practice appears to have been prevalent in some parts of India from a very ancient time. The *Shushruta'*, a work on medicine some two thousand years old, describes the wounding of the lingam with the teeth as one of the causes of a disease treated upon in that work. Traces of the practice are found as far back as the eighth century, for various kind of the Auparishtaka are represented in the sculptures of many Shaivite temples at Bhubaneshwar, near Cuttack, in Orissa, which were built about that period. From these sculptures being found in such places, it would seem that this practice was popular in that part of the country at that time. It does not seem to be so prevalent now in Hindustan, its place perhaps being supplanted by the practice of sodomy introduced since the Muslim period.

kind embraces and draws toward himself the thighs of the man whom he is shampooing, and after this he touches the joints of the thighs and the jaghana, or central portions, of the body. Then, if he finds the lingam of the man erect, he presses it with his hands, and chaffs him for getting into that state. If after this, and after knowing the eunuch's intention, the man does not tell the eunuch to proceed, then the latter does it of his own accord and begins the congress. If, however, he is ordered by the man to do it, then he disputes with him, and consents at last, but only with difficulty.

The following eight things are then done by the eunuch one after the other:

> The nominal congress
> Biting the sides
> Pressing outside
> Pressing inside
> Kissing
> Rubbing
> Sucking a mango fruit
> Swallowing up

At the end of each of these, the eunuch expresses his wish to stop; but when one of them is finished, the man desires him to do another, and after that is done, then the one that follows it, and so on.

(1). When, holding the man's lingam with his hand, and placing it between his lips, the eunuch moves his mouth about, it is called the "nominal congress."

(2). When, covering the end of the lingam with his fingers collected together like the bud of a plant or flower, the eunuch presses the sides of it with his lips, using his teeth also, it is called "biting the sides."

(3). When, being desired to proceed, the eunuch presses the end of the lingam with his lips closed together, and kisses it as if he were drawing it out, it is called the "outside pressing."

(4). When, being asked to go on, he puts the lingam further into his mouth, and presses it with his lips and then takes it out, it is called the "inside pressing."

(5). When, holding the lingam in his hand, the eunuch kisses it as if he were kissing the lower lip, it is called "pressing."

(6). When, after kissing it, he touches it with his tongue everywhere, and passes his tongue over the end of it, it is called "rubbing."

(7). When, in the same way, he puts the half of it into his mouth, and forcibly kisses and sucks it, this is called "sucking a mango fruit."

(8). And, lastly, when with the consent of the man the eunuch puts the whole lingam into his mouth, and presses it to the very end, as if he were going to swallow it up, it is called "swallowing up."

Striking, scratching, and other things may also be done during this kind of congress.

The Auparishtaka is practiced also by unchaste and wanton women, female attendants, and serving maids, that is, those who are not married to anybody, but who live by shampooing.

The Acharyas (ancient and venerable authors) are of opinion that this Auparishtaka is the work of a dog and of a man, because it is a low practice, and opposed to the orders of the Holy Writ (Dharma Shastras), and because the man himself suffers by bringing his lingam into contact with the mouths of eunuchs and women. But Vatsyayana says that the orders of the Holy Writ do not affect those who resort to courtesans, and the law prohibits the practice of the Auparishtaka with married women only. As regards the injury to the male, that can be easily remedied.

The people of eastern India do not resort to women who practice the Auparishtaka.

The people of Ahichhatra resort to such women, but do nothing with them so far as the mouth is concerned.

The people of Saketa do with these women every kind of

mouth congress, while the people of Nagara do not practice this, but do every other thing.

The people of the Shurasena country, on the southern bank of the Jumna, do everything without any hesitation, for they say that women being naturally unclean, no one can be certain about their character, their purity, their conduct, their practices, their confidences, or their speech. They are not, however, on this account to be abandoned, because religious law, on the authority of which they are reckoned pure, lays down that the udder of a cow is clean at the time of milking, though the mouth of a cow, and also the mouth of her calf, are considered unclean by the Hindus. Again, a dog is clean when he seizes a deer in hunting, though food touched by a dog is otherwise considered very unclean. A bird is clean when it causes a fruit to fall from a tree by pecking at it, though things eaten by crows and other birds are considered unclean. And the mouth of a woman is clean for kissing and suchlike things at the time of sexual intercourse. Vatsyayana, moreover, thinks that in all these things connected with love, everybody should act according to the custom of his country, and his own inclination.

There are also the following verses on the subject:

"The male servants of some men carry on the mouth congress with their masters. It is also practiced by some citizens, who know each other well, among themselves. Some women of the harem, when they are amorous, do the acts of the mouth on the yonis of one another, and some men do the same thing with women. The way of doing this (kissing the yoni) should be known from kissing the mouth. When a man and woman lie down in an inverted order, with the head of the one toward the feet of the other, and carry on this congress, it is called the "congress of a crow."

For the sake of such things, courtesans abandon men possessed of good qualities, liberal and clever, and become attached to low persons, such as slaves and elephant drivers. The Auparishtaka, or mouth congress, should never be done by a learned Brahman, by a minister that carries on the business of a state, or by a man of good reputation, because though the practice is allowed by the Shastras, there is no reason why it should be carried on, and need be practiced only in particular cases. For instance, the taste and the digestive qualities of the flesh of dogs are mentioned in works on medicine, but it does not therefore follow that it should be eaten by the wise. In the same way there are some men, some places, and some times with respect to which these practices can be made use of. A man should therefore pay regard to the place, to the time, and to the practice which is to be carried out, as also as to whether it is agreeable to his nature and to himself, and then he may or may not practice these things according to circumstances. But after all, these things being done secretly, and the mind of the man being fickle, how can it be known what any person will do at any particular time and for any particular purpose?

## Chapter X

*How to Begin and How to End the Congress;
Different Kinds of Congress, and Love Quarrels*

In the pleasure room, decorated with flowers, and fragrant with perfumes, attended by his friends and servants, the citizen should receive the woman, who will come bathed and dressed, and will invite her to take refreshment and to drink freely. He should then seat her on his left side, and holding her hair, and touching also the end and knot of her garment, he should gently embrace her with his right arm. They should then carry on an amusing conversation on various subjects, and may also talk suggestively of things which would be considered as coarse, or not to be mentioned generally in society. They may then sing, either with or without gesticulations, and play on musical instruments, talk about the arts, and persuade each other to drink. At last, when the woman is overcome with love and desire, the citizen should dismiss the people that may be with him, giving them flowers, ointments, and betel leaves; and then when the two are left alone, they should proceed as has been already described in the previous chapters.

Such is the beginning of sexual union. At the end of the congress, the lovers, with modesty, and not looking at each other, should go separately to the washing room. After this, sitting in their own places, they should eat some betel leaves, and the citizen should apply with his own hand to the body of the woman some pure sandalwood ointment, or ointment of some other kind. He should then embrace her with his left arm, and with agreeable words should cause her to drink from a cup held in his own hand, or he may give her water to drink. They can then eat sweatmeats, or anything else, according to their liking, and may drink fresh juice,[1] soup, gruel, extracts of meat, sherbet, the juice of mango fruits, the extract of the juice of the citron tree mixed with sugar, or anything that may be liked in different countries, and known to be sweet, soft, and pure. The lovers may also sit on the terrace of the palace or house, and enjoy the moonlight, and carry on an agreeable conversation. At this time, too, while the woman lies in his lap, with her face toward the moon, the citizen should show her the different planets, the morning star, the polar star, and the seven Rishis, or Great Bear.

This is the end of sexual union.

Congress is of the following kinds:

> Loving congress
> Congress of subsequent love
> Congress of artificial love
> Congress of transferred love
> Congress like that of eunuchs
> Deceitful congress
> Congress of spontaneous love

(1). When a man and a woman who have been in love with each other for some time come together with great difficulty, or when one of the two returns from a journey, or is reconciled after having been separated because of a quarrel, then congress is called the "loving congress." It is carried on according to the liking of the lovers, and for as long as they choose.

---

[1] The fresh juice of the coconut tree, the date tree, and other kinds of palm trees are drunk in India. It will not keep fresh very long, but ferments rapidly, and is then distilled into liquor.

(2). When two persons come together, while their love for each other is still in its infancy, their congress is called the "congress of subsequent love."

(3). When a man carries on the congress by exciting himself by means of the sixty-four ways, such as kissing, and so on, or when a man and a woman come together, though in reality they are both attached to different persons, their congress is then called "congress of artificial love." At this time all the ways and means mentioned in the *Kama Shastra* should be used.

(4). When a man, from the beginning to the end of the congress, though having connection with the woman, thinks all the time he is enjoying another one whom he loves, it is called the "congress of transferred love."

(5). Congress between a man and a female water carrier, or a female servant of a caste lower than his own, lasting only until the desire is satisfied, is called "congress like that of eunuchs." Here external touches, kisses, and manipulations are not to be employed.

(6). The congress between a courtesan and a rustic, and that between citizens and the women of villages and bordering countries, are called "deceitful congress."

(7). The congress that takes place between two persons who are attached to one another, and which is done according to their own liking, is called "spontaneous congress."

Thus ends discourse of the kinds of congress.

We shall now speak of love quarrels.

A woman who is very much in love with a man cannot bear to hear the name of her rival mentioned, or to have any conversation regarding her, or to be addressed by her name through mistake. If such takes place, a great quarrel arises, and the woman cries, becomes angry, tosses her hair about, strikes her lover, falls from her bed or seat, and, casting aside her garlands and ornaments, throws herself down on the ground.

At this time the lover should attempt to reconcile her

with conciliatory words, and should take her up carefully and place her on her bed. But she, not replying to his questions, and with increased anger, should bend down his head by pulling his hair, and having kicked him once, twice, or thrice on his arms, head, bosom, or back, should then proceed to the door of the room. Dattaka says that she should then sit angrily near the door and shed tears, but should not go out, because she would be found fault with for going away. After a time, when she thinks that the conciliatory words and actions of her lover have reached their utmost, she should then embrace him, talking to him with harsh and reproachful words, but at the same time showing a loving desire for congress.

When the woman is in her own house, and has quarreled with her lover, she should go to him and show how angry she is, and leave him. Afterward the citizen having sent the Vita, the Vidushaka, or the Pithamarda to pacify her, she should accompany them back to the house, and spend the night with her lover.

Thus ends discourse of the love quarrels.

In conclusion:

A man employing the sixty-four means mentioned by Babhravya obtains his object, and enjoys the woman of the first quality. Though he may speak well on other subjects, if he does not know sixty-four divisions, no great respect is paid to him in the assembly of the learned. A man, devoid of other knowledge, but well acquainted with the sixty-four divisions, becomes a leader in any society of men and women. What man will not respect the sixty-four parts, considering they are respected by the learned, by the cunning, and by the courtesans? As the sixty-four parts are respected, are charming, and add to the talent of women, they are called by the Acharyas dear to women. A man skilled in the sixty-four parts is looked upon with love by his own wife, by the wives of others, and by courtesans.

# PART THREE

*About the Acquisition of a Wife*

———

## Chapter 1

### On Marriage

When a girl of the same caste, and a virgin, is married in accordance with the precepts of Holy Writ (Dharma Shastras), the results of such a union are: the acquisition of Dharma and Artha, offspring, affinity, increase of friends, and untarnished love. For this reason a man should fix his affections upon a girl who is of good family, whose parents are alive, and who is three years or more younger than himself. She should be born of a highly respectable family, possessed of wealth, well connected, and with many relations and friends. She should also be beautiful, of a good disposition, with lucky marks on her body, and with good hair, nails, teeth, ears, eyes, and breasts, neither more nor less than they ought to be, and no one of them entirely wanting, and not troubled with a sickly body. The man should, of course, also possess these qualities himself. But at all events, says Ghotakamukha, a girl who has been already joined with others (that is, no longer a maiden) should never be loved, for it would be reproachful to do such a thing.

Now, in order to bring about a marriage with a girl such as described above, the parents and relations of the man should exert themselves, as should such friends on both sides as may be desired to assist in the matter. These friends should bring to the notice of the girl's parents, the faults, both present and future, of all the other men that may wish to marry her,

135

and should at the same time extol even to exaggeration all
the excellences, ancestral and paternal, of their friend, so as
to endear him to them, and particularly to those that may be
liked by the girl's mother. One of the friends should also
disguise himself as an astrologer, and declare the future good
fortune and wealth of his friend by showing the existence of
all the lucky omens [1] and signs,[2] the good influence of
planets, the auspicious entrance of the sun into a sign of the
Zodiac, propitious stars and fortunate marks on his body.
Others again should rouse the jealousy of the girl's mother
by telling her that their friend has a chance of getting from
some other quarter an even better girl than hers.

A girl should be taken as a wife, and given in marriage,
when fortune, signs, omens, and the words [3] of others are
favorable, for, says Ghotakamukha, a man should not marry
at any time he likes. A girl who is asleep, crying, or gone out
of the house when sought in marriage, or who is betrothed
to another, should not be married. The following should also
be avoided:

> One who is kept concealed
> One who has an ill-sounding name
> One who has her nose depressed
> One who has her nostril turned up
> One who is formed like a male
> One who is bent down

[1] The flight of a bluejay on a person's left is considered a lucky omen
when one starts on any business; the appearance of a cat before anyone at such a time is looked on as a bad omen. There are many omens
of the same kind.

[2] Such as the throbbing of the right eye of men and the left eye of
women, etc.

[3] Before anything is begun it is a custom to go early in the morning to a neighbor's house, and overhear the first words that may be
spoken in his family, and according as the words heard are of good
or bad import, so draw an inference as to the success or failure of the
undertaking.

One who has crooked thighs
One who has a projecting forehead
One who has a bald head
One who does not like purity
One who has been polluted by another
One who is affected with the Gulma [4]
One who is disfigured in any way
One who has fully arrived at puberty
One who is a friend
One who is a younger sister
One who is a Varshakari [5]

In the same way a girl who is called by the name of one of the twenty-seven stars, or by the name of a tree, or of a river, is considered worthless, as also a girl whose name ends in "r" or "l." But some authors say that prosperity is gained only by marrying that girl to whom one becomes attached and that therefore no other girl but the one who is loved should be married by anyone.

When a girl becomes marriageable her parents should dress her smartly, and should place her where she can be easily seen by all. Every afternoon, having dressed her and decorated her in a becoming manner, they should send her with her female companions to sports, sacrifices, and marriage ceremonies, and thus show her to advantage in society, because she is a kind of merchandise. They should also receive with kind words and signs of friendliness those of an auspicious appearance who may come accompanied by their friends and relatives for the purpose of marrying the daughter; and, under some pretext or other having first dressed her becomingly, the parents should then present her to them. After this, they should await the pleasure of fortune, and with this object should appoint a

[4] A disease consisting of any glandular enlargement in any part of the body.
[5] A woman the palms of whose hands and the soles of whose feet are always perspiring.

future day on which a determination could be come to with regard to their daughter's marriage. On this occasion when the persons have come, the parents of the girl should ask them to bathe ana dine, and should say, "Everything will take place at the proper time," and should not then comply with the request, but should settle the matter later.

When a girl is thus acquired, either according to the custom of the country or according to his own desire, the man should marry her in accordance with the precepts of the Holy Writ, according to one of the four kinds of marriage.

Thus ends discourse of marriage.

There are also some verses on the subject, as follows:

"Amusement in society, such as completing verses begun by others, marriages, and auspicious ceremonies, should be carried on neither with superiors nor with inferiors, but with our equals. That should be known as a high connection when a man, after marrying a girl, has to serve her and her relatives afterward like a servant, and such a connection is censured by the good. On the other hand, that reproachable connection where a man, together with his relatives, lords it over his wife is called a low connection by the wise. But when both the man and the woman afford mutual pleasure to each other, and where the relatives on both sides pay respect to one another, such is called a connection in the proper sense of the word. Therefore a man should contract neither a high connection by which he is obliged to bow down afterward to his kinsmen, nor a low connection, which is universally reprehended by all."

## Chapter II

### On Creating Confidence in the Girl

For the first three days after marriage, the girl and her husband should sleep on the floor, abstain from sexual pleasures, and eat their food without seasoning it either with alkali or salt. For the next seven days they should bathe amidst the sounds of auspicious musical instruments, should decorate themselves, dine together, and pay attention to their relatives as well as to those who may have come to witness their marriage. This is applicable to persons of all castes. On the night of the tenth day the man should begin in a lonely place with soft words, and thus create confidence in the girl. Some authors say that for the purpose of winning her over he should not speak to her for three days; but the followers of Babhravya are of the opinion that if the man does not speak with her for three days, the girl may be discouraged by seeing him spiritless, like a pillar, and, becoming dejected, she may begin to despise him as a eunuch. Vatsyayana says that the man should begin to win her over, and to create confidence in her, but should abstain at first from sexual pleasures. Women being of a tender nature, want tender beginnings, and when they are forcibly approached by men with whom they are but slightly acquainted, they sometimes suddenly become haters of sexual connection, and sometimes even haters of the male sex. The man should therefore approach the girl according to her liking, and should make use of those devices by which he may be able to establish himself more and more in her confidence. These devices are as follows:

He should embrace her first of all in the law she likes most, because it does not last for a long time.

He should embrace her with the upper part of his body, because that is easier and simpler. If the girl is grown up, or if the man has known her for some time, he may embrace her by the light of a lamp; but if he is not well acquainted with her, or if she is a young girl, he should then embrace her in darkness.

When the girl accepts the embrace, the man should put a "tambula," or screw of betel nut and betel leaves, in her mouth, and if she will not take it, he should induce her to do so by conciliatory words, entreaties, oaths, and kneeling at her feet, for it is a universal rule that however bashful or angry a woman may be, she never disregards a man's kneeling at her feet. At the time of giving this tambula, he should kiss her mouth softly and gracefully, without making any sound. When she is gained over in this respect, he should then make her talk, and so that she may be induced to talk he should ask her questions about things of which he knows or pretends to know nothing, and which can be answered in a few words. If she does not speak to him, he should not frighten her, but should ask her the same thing again and again in a conciliatory manner. If she does not then speak, he should urge her to give a reply, because, as Ghotakamukha says, "All girls hear everything said to them by men, but do not themselves sometimes say a single word." When she is thus importuned, the girl should give replies by shakes of the head, but if she quarreled with the man she should not even do that. When she is asked by the man whether she desires him, and whether she likes him, she should remain silent for a long time, and when at last importuned to reply, should give him a favorable answer by a nod of her head. If the man is previously acquainted with the girl, he should converse with her by means of a female friend, who may be favorable to him, and in the confidence of both, and carry on the conversation on both sides. On such an occasion the girl should smile with her head bent down, and if the female friend say more on her part than she was desired to do, she should chide her and dispute with her. The female friend should say in jest even what she is not desired to say by the girl, and add, "She says so"; on which the girl should say, indistinctly and prettily, "Oh, no! I did not say so," and she should then smile, and throw an occasional glance toward the man.

If the girl is familiar with the man, she should place near him, without saying anything, the tambula, the ointment, or the garland that he may have asked for, or she may tie them up in his upper garment. While she is engaged in this, the man should touch her young breasts in the sounding way of pressing with the nails, and if she prevents him doing this he should say to her, "I will not do it again if you will embrace me," and should in this way cause her to embrace him. While he is being embraced by her he should pass his hand repeatedly over and about her body. By and by he should place her in his lap, and try more and more to gain her consent, and if she will not yield to him he should frighten her by saying: "I shall impress marks of my teeth and nails on your lips and breasts, and then make similar marks on my own body, and shall tell my friends that you did them. What will you say then?" In this and other ways, as fear and confidence are created in the minds of children, so should the man gain her over to his wishes.

On the second and third nights, after her confidence has increased still more, he should feel the whole of her body with his hands, and kiss her all over; he should also place his hands upon her thighs and shampoo them, and if he succeeds in this he should then shampoo the joints of her thighs. If she tries to prevent him doing this, he should say to her, "What harm is there in doing it?" and should persuade her to let him do it. After gaining this point he should touch her private parts, should loosen her girdle and the knot of her dress, and, turning up her lower garment, should shampoo the joints of her naked thighs. Under various pretenses he should do all these things, but he should not at that time begin actual congress. After this, he should teach her the sixty-four arts, should tell her how much he loves her, and describe to her the hopes he formerly entertained regarding her. He should also promise to be faithful to her in future, and should dispel all her fears with respect to rival women, and at last, after having overcome her bashfulness, he should begin to enjoy her in a way so as not to frighten her. So much about creating confidence in the girl; there are, moreover, some verses on the subject, as follows:

"A man acting according to the inclinations of a girl should try to gain her over so that she may love him and place her confidence in him. A man does not succeed either by implicity following the inclination of a girl or by wholly opposing her, and he should therefore adopt a middle course. He who knows how to make himself beloved by women, as well as to increase their honor and create confidence in them, becomes an object of their love. But he who neglects a girl, thinking she is too bashful, is despised by her as a beast ignorant of the working of the female mind. Moreover, a girl forcibly enjoyed by one who does not understand the hearts of girls become nervous, uneasy, and dejected, and suddenly begins to hate the man who has taken advantage of her; and then, when her love is not understood or returned, she sinks into despondency, and becomes either a hater of mankind altogether or, hating her own man, she has recourse to other men.

## Chapter III

### On Courtship, and the Manifestation of the
### Feelings by Outward Signs and Deeds

A poor man possessed of good qualities, a man born of a low family possessed of mediocre qualities, a neighbor possessed of wealth, and one under the control of his father, mother, or brothers, should not marry without endeavoring to gain over the girl from her childhood to love and esteem them. Thus a boy separated from his parents, and living in the house of his uncle, should try to gain over the daughter of his uncle, or some other girl, even though she be previously betrothed to another. And this way of gaining over a girl, says Ghota-kamukha, is unexceptionable, because Dharma can be accomplished by means of it, as well as by any other way of marriage.

When a boy has thus begun to woo the girl he loves, he should spend his time with her and amuse her with various games and diversions fitted for their age and acquaintanceship, such as picking and collecting flowers, making garlands of flowers, playing the parts of members of a fictitious family, cooking food, playing with dice, playing with cards, the game of odd and even, the game of finding out the middle finger, the game of six pebbles, and such other games as may be prevalent in the country, and agreeable to the disposition of the girl. In addition to this, he should carry on various amusing games played by several persons together, such as hide-and-seek, playing with seeds, hiding things in several small heaps of wheat and looking for them, blind-man's buff, gymnastic exercises, and other games of the same sort in company with the girl, her friends, and female attendants. The man should also show great kindness to any woman whom the girl thinks fit to be trusted, and should also make new acquaintances, but above all he should attach to himself by kindness and little services the daughter of the girl's nurse, for if she be gained over, even though she comes to know of his design, she does not cause any obstruction, but is sometimes even able to effect a union between him and the girl. And though she knows the true character of the man, she always talks of his many excellent qualities to the parents and relations of the girl, even though she may not be desired to do so by him.

In this way the man should do whatever the girl takes most delight in, and he should get for her whatever she may have a desire to possess. Thus he should procure for her such play-things as may be hardly known to other girls. He may also show her a ball dyed with various colors, and other curiosities of the same sort; and should give her dolls made of cloth, wood, buffalo horn, ivory, wax, flour, or earth; also utensils for cooking food; and figures in wood, such as a man and woman standing, a pair of rams or goats or sheep; also temples made of earth, bamboo, or wood, dedicated to various goddesses, and cages for parrots, cuckoos, starlings, quails, cocks, and partridges; water vessels of different sorts and of elegant forms, machines for throwing water about, guitars, stands for putting images upon, stools, lac, red arsenic, yellow ointment, vermilion and collyrium, as well as sandalwood, saffron, betel nut and betel leaves. Such things should be given at different times whenever he gets a good opportunity of meeting her in public, according to circumstances. In short, he should try in every way to make her look upon him as one who would do for her everything that she wanted to be done.

In the next place he should get her to meet him in some place privately, and should then tell her that the reason for his giving presents to her in secret was the fear that the parents of both of them might be displeased, and then he may add that the things which he had given her had been much desired by other people. When her love begins to show signs of increasing, he should relate to her agreeable stories if she expresses a wish to hear such narratives. Or if she takes delight in legerdemain, he should amaze her by performing various tricks of jugglery; or if she feels a great curiosity to see a performance of the various arts, he should show his own skill in them. When she is delighted with singing, he should entertain her with music, and on certain days, and at the time of going together to moonlight fairs and festivals, and at the time of her return after being absent from home, he should present her with bouquets of flowers and with chaplets for the head and with ear ornaments and rings, for these are the proper occasions on which such things should be presented.

He should also teach the daughter of the girl's nurse all the sixty-four means of pleasure practiced by men, and under this pretext should also inform her of his great skill in the art of sexual enjoyment. All this time he should wear a fine dress, and make as good an appearance as possible, for young women love men who live with them, and who are handsome, good looking, and well dressed. As for the saying that though women may fall in love, they still make no effort themselves to gain over the object of their affections, that is only a matter of idle talk.

Now, a girl always shows her love by outward signs and actions such as the following: She never looks the man in the face, and becomes abashed when she is looked at by him; under some pretext or other she shows her limbs to him; she looks secretly at him, though he has gone away from her side; hangs down her head when she is asked some question by him, and answers in indistinct words and unfinished sentences, delights to be in his company for a long time, speaks to her attendants in a peculiar tone with the hope of attracting his attention toward her when she is at a distance from him, and does not wish to go from the place where he is; under some pretext or other she makes him look at different things, narrates to him tales and stories very slowly so that she may continue conversing with him for a long time; kisses and embraces before him a child sitting in her lap; draws ornamental marks on the foreheads of her female servants, performs sportive and graceful movements when her attendants speak jestingly to her in the presence of her lover; confides in her lover's friends, and respects and obeys them; shows kindness to his servants, converses with them and engages them to do her work as if she were their mistress, and listens attentively to them when they tell stories about her lover to somebody else; enters his house when induced to do so by the daughter of her nurse, and by her assistance manages to converse and play with him; avoids being seen by her lover when she is not dressed and decorated; gives him by the hand of her female friend her ear ornament, ring, or garland of flowers that he may have asked to see; always wears anything that he may have presented to her, becomes dejected when any other bridegroom is mentioned by her parents, and does not mix with those who may be of his party, or who may support his claims.

There are also some verses on the subject, as follows:

"A man who has seen and perceived the feelings of the girl toward him, and who has noticed the outward signs and movements by which those feelings are expressed, should do everything in his power to effect a union with her. He should gain over a young girl by childlike sports; a damsel come of age by his skill in the arts, and a girl that loves him, by having recourse to persons in whom she confides."

## Chapter IV

*On Things to Be Done Only by the Man, and the
Acquisition of the Girl Thereby. Also, What Is to
Be Done by a Girl to Gain Over a Man, and Subject
Him to Her*

Now, when the girl begins to show her love by outward signs
and motions, as described in the last chapter, the lover should
try to gain her over entirely by various ways and means, such
as the following:

When engaged with her in any game or sport, he should
intentionally hold her hand. He should practice upon her the
various kinds of embraces, such as the touching embrace, and
others already described in a preceding chapter (Part Two,
Chapter II). He should show her a pair of human beings cut
out of the leaf of a tree, and suchlike things, at intervals.
When engaged in water sports, he should dive at a distance
from her, and come up close to her. He should show an increased liking for the new foliage of trees and suchlike things.
He should describe to her the pangs he suffers on her account.
He should relate to her the beautiful dream that he has had
with reference to other women. At parties and assemblies of
his caste he should sit near her, and touch her under some
pretense or other, and having placed his foot upon hers, he
should slowly touch each of her toes, and press the ends of the
nails; if successful in this, he should get hold of her foot with
his hand and repeat the same thing. He should also press a
finger of her hand between his toes when she happens to be
washing his feet; and whenever he gives anything to her or

takes anything from her, he should show her by his manner and looks how much he loves her.

He should sprinkle upon her the water brought for rinsing his mouth; and when alone with her in a lonely place, or in darkness, he should make love to her, and tell her the true state of his mind without distressing her in any way.

Whenever he sits with her on the same seat or bed he should say to her, "I have something to tell you in private," and then, when she comes to hear it in a quiet place, he should express his love to her more by manner and signs than by words. When he comes to know the state of her feelings toward him, he should pretend to be ill, and should make her come to his house to speak to him. There he should intentionally hold her hand and place it on his eyes and forehead, and under the pretense of preparing some medicine for him he should ask her to do the work for his sake in the following words: "This work must be done by you, and by nobody else." When she wants to go away he should let her go, with an earnest request to come and see him again. This device of illness should be continued for three days and three nights. After this, when she begins coming to see him frequently, he should carry on long conversations with her, for, says Ghotakamukha, "though a man loves a girl ever so much, he never succeeds in winning her without a great deal of talking." At last, when the man finds the girl completely won over, he may then begin to enjoy her. As for the saying that women grow less timid than usual during the evening, at night, and in darkness, and are desirous of congress at those times, and do not oppose men then, and should only be enjoyed at these hours, it is a matter of talk only.

When it is impossible for the man to carry on his endeavors alone, he should, by means of the daughter of her nurse, or of a female friend in whom she confides, cause the girl to be brought to him without making known to her his design, and he should then proceed with her in the manner above described.

Or he should in the beginning send his own female servant to live with the girl as her friend, and should then gain her over by her means.

At last, when he knows the state of her feeling by her outward manner and conduct toward him at religious ceremonies, marriage ceremonies, fairs, festivals, theaters, public assemblies, and suchlike occasions, he should begin to enjoy her when she is alone, for Vatsyayana lays it down that women, when resorted to at proper times and in proper places, do not turn away from their lovers.

When a girl, possessed of good qualities and well bred, though born of a humble family, or destitute of wealth, and not therefore desired by her equals, or an orphan girl, or one deprived of her parents, but observing the rules of her family and caste, wishes to bring about her own marriage when she comes of age, such a girl should endeavor to gain over a strong and good-looking young man or a person whom she thinks would marry her on account of the weakness of his mind, and even without the consent of his parents. She should do this by such means as would endear her to the said person, as well as by frequently seeing and meeting him. Her mother also should constantly cause them to meet by means of her female friends, and the daughter of her nurse. The girl herself should try to get alone with her beloved in some quiet place, and at odd times should give him flowers, betel nut, betel leaves, and perfumes. She should also show her skill in the practice of the arts, in shampooing, in scratching and in pressing with the nails. She should also talk to him on the subjects he likes best, and discuss with him the ways and means of gaining over and winning the affections of a girl.

But old authors say that although the girl loves the man ever so much, she should not offer herself, or make the first overtures, for a girl who does this loses her dignity, and is liable to be scorned and rejected. But when the man shows his wish to enjoy her, she should be favorable to him, and should show no change in her demeanor when he embraces her, and should receive all the manifestations of his love as if she were ignorant of the state of his mind. But when he tries to kiss her she should oppose him; when he begs to be allowed to have sexual intercourse with her she should let him touch her private parts only and with considerable difficulty; and though importuned by him, she should not yield herself up to him as if of her own accord, but should resist his attempts to have her. Moreover, it is only when she is certain that she is truly loved and that her lover is indeed devoted to her, and will not change his mind, that she should then give herself up to him, and persuade him to marry her quickly. After losing her virginity she should tell her confidential friends about it.

Here ends discourse of the efforts of a girl to gain over a man.

There are also some verses on the subject, as follows:

"A girl who is much sought after should marry the man she likes, and whom she thinks would be obedient to her, and capable of giving her pleasure. But when from the desire of wealth a girl is married by her parents to a rich man without taking into consideration the character or looks of the bridegroom, or when given to a man who has several wives, she never becomes attached to the man, even though he be endowed with good qualities, obedient to her will, active, strong, and healthy, and anxious to please her in every way. A husband who is obedient but yet master of himself, though he be poor and not good looking, is better than one who is common to many women, even though he be handsome and attractive. The wives of rich men, where there are many wives, are not generally attached to their husbands, and are not confidential with them, and even though they possess all the external enjoyments of life, still have recourse to other men. A man who is of a low mind, who has fallen from his social position, and who is much given to traveling, does not deserve to be married; neither does one who has many wives and children, or one who is devoted to sport and gambling, and who comes to his wife only when he likes. Of all the lovers of a girl, he only is her true husband who possesses the qualities that are liked by her, and such a husband enjoys real superiority over her only because he is the husband of love."

## Chapter V

### On Certain Forms of Marriage [1]

When a girl cannot meet her lover frequently in private, she should send the daughter of her nurse to him, it being understood that she has confidence in her, and had previously gained her over to her interests. On seeing the man, the daughter of the nurse should, in the course of conversation, describe to him the noble birth, the good disposition, the beauty, talent, skill, knowledge of human nature, and affection of the girl in such a way as not to let him suppose that she had been sent by the girl, and should thus create affection for the girl in the heart of the man. To the girl also she should speak about the excellent qualities of the man, especially of those qualities which she knows are pleasing to the girl. She should, moreover, speak with disparagement of the other lovers of the girl, and talk about the avarice and indiscretion of their parents, and the fickleness of their relations. She should also quote samples of many girls of ancient times, such as Sakuntala and others who, having united themselves with lovers of their own caste and their own choice, were happy ever afterward in their society. She should also tell of other girls who married into great families, and being troubled by rival

[1] These forms of marriage differ from the four kinds of marriage mentioned in Part Three, Chapter I, and are only to be made use of when the girl is gained over in the way mentioned in Chapters III and IV.

wives became wretched and miserable, and were finally abandoned. She should further speak of the good fortune, the continual happiness, the chastity, obedience, and affection of the man; and if the girl gets amorous about him, she should endeavor to allay her shame and her fear, as well as her suspicions about any disaster that might result from her marriage. In a word, she should act the whole part of a female messenger by telling the girl all about the man's affection for her, the places he frequented, and the endeavors he made to meet her, and by frequently repeating, "It will be all right if the man takes you away forcibly and unexpectedly."

## The Forms of Marriage

When the girl is gained over, and acts openly with the man as his wife, he should cause fire to be brought from the house of a Brahman, and having spread the Kusha grass upon the ground, and offered an oblation to the fire, he should marry her according to the precepts of the religious law. After this he should inform his parents of the fact, because it is the opinion of ancient authors that a marriage solemnly contracted in the presence of fire cannot afterward be set aside.

After the consummation of the marriage, the relations of the man should gradually be made acquainted with the affair, and the relations of the girl should also be apprised of it in such a way that they may consent to the marriage, and overlook the manner in which it was brought about, and when this is done they should afterward be reconciled by affectionate presents and favorable conduct. In this manner the man should marry the girl according to the Gandharva form of marriage.

When the girl cannot make up her mind, or will not express her readiness to marry, the man should obtain her in any one of the following ways:

1. On a fitting occasion, and under some excuse, he should, by means of a female friend with whom he is well acquainted and whom he can trust, and who also is well known to the girl's family, get the girl brought unexpectedly to his house,

and he should then bring fire from the house of a Brahman, and proceed as before described.

2. When the marriage of the girl with some other person draws near, the man should disparage the future husband to the utmost in the mind of the mother of the girl, and then, having got the girl to come with her mother's consent to a neighboring house, he should bring fire from the house of a Brahman, and proceed as above.

3. The man should become a great friend of the brother of the girl, the said brother being of the same age as himself, and addicted to courtesans and to intrigues with the wives of other people, and should give him assistance in such matters, and also give him occasional presents. He should then tell him about his great love for his sister, as young men will sacrifice even their lives for the sake of those who may be of the same age, habits, and dispositions as themselves. After this the man should have the girl brought by means of her brother to some secure place, and, having brought fire from the house of a Brahman, should proceed as before.

4. The man should on the occasion of festivals get the daughter of the nurse to give the girl some intoxicating substance, and then cause her to be brought to some secure place under the pretense of some business, and there having enjoyed her before she recovers from her intoxication, should bring fire from the house of a Brahman, and proceed as before.

5. The man should, with the connivance of the daughter of the nurse, carry off the girl from her house while she is asleep, and then, having enjoyed her before she recovers from her sleep, should bring fire from the house of a Brahman, and proceed as before.

6. When the girl goes to a garden, or to some village in the neighborhood, the man should, with his friends, fall on her guards, and having killed them or frightened them away, forcibly carry her off, and proceed as before.

There are verses on this subject as follows:

"In all the forms of marriage given in this chapter of this

work, the one that precedes is better than the one that follows it on account of its being more in accordance with the commands of religion, and therefore it is only when it is impossible to carry the former into practice that the latter should be resorted to. As the fruit of all good marriages is love, the Gandharva [2] form of marriage is respected, even though it is formed under unfavorable circumstances, because it fulfills the object sought for. Another cause of the respect accorded to the Gandharva form of marriage is that it brings forth happiness, causes less trouble in its performance than the other forms of marriage, and is above all the result of previous love."

[2] About the Gandharvavivaha form of marriage, see note to page 28 of Sir R. F. Burton's *Vickram and the Vampire: or, Tales of Hindu Devilry* (Longmans, Green & Co., London, 1870): "This form of matrimony was recognised by the ancient Hindus, and is frequent in books. It is a kind of Scotch wedding—ultra-Caledonian—taking place by mutual consent without any form or ceremony. The Gandharvas are heavenly minstrels of Indra's court, who are supposed to be witnesses."

# PART FOUR

*About a Wife*

## Chapter I

### On the Manner of Living of a Virtuous Woman, and of Her Behavior During the Absence of Her Husband

A virtuous woman, who has affection for her husband, should act in conformity with his wishes as if he were a divine being, and with his consent should take upon herself the whole care of his family. She should keep the whole house well cleaned, and arrange flowers of various kinds in different parts of it, and make the floor smooth and polished so as to give the whole a neat and becoming appearance. She should surround the house with a garden, and place ready in it all the materials required for the morning, noon, and evening sacrifices. Moreover, she should herself revere the sanctuary of the household gods, for, says Gonardiya, "Nothing so much attracts the heart of a householder to his wife as a careful observance of the things mentioned above."

Toward the parents, relations, friends, sisters, and servants of her husband she should behave as they deserve. In the garden she should plant beds of green vegetables, bunches of the sugar cane, and clumps of the fig tree, the mustard plant, the parsley plant, the fennel plant, and the *Xanthochymus pictorius*. Clusters of various flowers, such as the *Trapa bispinosa*, the jasmine, the *Jasminum grandiflorum*, the yellow amaranth, the wild jasmine, the *Tabernaemontana coronaria*, the nadyawort, the China rose, and others, should likewise be planted, together with the fragrant grass *Andropogon schœnanthus* and the fragrant root of the plant *Andropogon miricatus.* She should also have seats and arbors made in the garden, in the middle of which a well, tank, or pool should be dug.

The wife should always avoid the company of female beggars, female Buddhist mendicants, unchaste and roguish women, female fortunetellers and witches. As regards meals, she should aways consider what her husband likes and dislikes, and what things are good for him, and what are injurious to him. When she hears the sound of his footsteps coming home she should at once get up, and be ready to do whatever he may command her, and either order her female servant to wash his feet, or wash them herself. When going anywhere with her husband she should put on her ornaments, and without his consent she should neither give nor accept invitations, or attend marriages and sacrifices, or sit in the company of female friends, or visit the temples of the Gods. And if she wants to engage in any kind of games or sports, she should not do it against his will. In the same way she should always sit down after him, and get up before him, and should never awaken him when he is asleep. The kitchen should be situated in a quiet and retired place, so as not to be accessible to strangers, and should always look clean.

In the event of any misconduct on the part of her husband, she should not blame him excessively, though she be a little displeased. She should not use abusive language toward him, but rebuke him with conciliatory words, whether he be in the company of friends or alone. Moreover, she should not be a scold, for, says Gonardiya "There is no cause of dislike on the part of a husband so great as this characteristic in a wife." Lastly, she should avoid bad expressions, sulky looks, speaking aside, standing in the doorway, and looking at passers-by, conversing in pleasure groves, and remaining in a lonely place for a long time; and finally she should always keep her body, her teeth, her hair, and everything belonging to her tidy, sweet, and clean.

When the wife wants to approach her husband in private,

her dress should consist of many ornaments, various kinds of flowers, and a cloth decorated with different colors, and some sweet-smelling ointments or unguents. But her everyday dress should be composed of a thin, close-textured cloth, a few ornaments and flowers, and a little scent, not too much. She should also observe the fasts and vows of her husband, and when he tries to prevent her doing this, she should persuade him to let her do it.

At appropriate times of the year, and when they happen to be cheap, she should buy earth, bamboos, firewood, skins, and iron pots, as well as salt and oil. Fragrant substances, vessels made of the fruit of the plant *Wrightea antidysenterica,* or oval-leaved *Wrightea,* medicines, and other things which are always wanted, should be obtained when required and kept in a secret place of the house. The seeds of the radish, the potato, the common beet, the Indian wormwood, the mango, the cucumber, the eggplant, the kushmanda, the pumpkin gourd, the surana, the *Bignonia indica,* the sandalwood, the *Premna spinosa,* the garlic plant, the onion, and other vegetables, should be bought and sown at the proper seasons.

The wife, moreover, should not tell to strangers the amount of her wealth, or the secrets which her husband has confided to her. She should surpass all the women of her own rank in life in her cleverness, her appearance, her knowledge of cookery, her pride, and her manner of serving her husband. The expenditure of the year should be regulated by the profits. The milk that remains after the meals should be turned into ghee, or clarified butter. Oil and sugar should be prepared at home: spinning and weaving should also be done there; and a store of ropes and cords, and barks of trees for twisting into ropes, should be kept. She should also attend to the pounding and cleaning of rice, using its small grain and chaff in some way or other. She should pay the salaries of the servants, look after the tilling of the fields, the keeping of the flocks and herds, superintend the making of vehicles, and take care of the rams, cocks, quails, parrots, starlings, cuckoos, peacocks, monkeys, and deer; and finally adjust the income and expenditure of the day. The worn-out clothes should be given to those servants who have done good work, in order to show them that their services have been appreciated, or they may be applied to some other use. The vessels in which wine is prepared, as well as those in which it is kept, should be carefully looked after, and put away at the proper time. All sales and purchases should also be well attended to. The friends of her husband she should welcome by presenting them with flowers, ointment, incense, betel leaves, and betel nut. Her father-in-law and mother-in-law she should treat as they deserve, always remaining dependent on their will, never contradicting them, speaking to them in few and not harsh words, not laughing loudly in their presence, and acting with their friends and enemies as with her own. In addition to the above she should not be vain, or too much taken up with her enjoyments. She should be liberal toward her servants, and reward them on holidays and festivals; and not give away anything without first making it known to her husband.

Thus ends discourse on the manner of a virtuous woman.

During the absence of her husband on a journey, the virtuous woman should wear only her auspicious ornaments, and observe the fasts in honor of the gods. While anxious to hear the news of her husband, she should still look after her household affairs. She should sleep near the elder women of the house, and make herself agreeable to them. She should look after and keep in repair the things that are liked by her husband, and continue the works that have been begun by him. To the abode of her relations she should not go except on occasions of joy and sorrow, and then she should go in her usual traveling dress, accompanied by her husband's servants, and not remain there for a long time. The fasts and feasts should be observed with the consent of the elders of the house. The resources should be increased by making purchases and sales according to the practice of the merchants, and by means of honest servants, superintended by herself. The income should be increased, and the expenditure diminished, as much as possible. And when her husband returns from his journey, she should receive him at first in her ordinary clothes, so that he may know in what way she has lived during his absence, and should bring to him some presents, as well as materials for the worship of the Deity.

Thus ends the part relating to the behavior of a wife during the absence of her husband on a journey.

There are also some verses on the subjects as follows:

"The wife, whether she be a woman of noble family or a virgin widow [1] remarried or a concubine, should lead a chaste life, devoted to her husband, and doing everything for his welfare. Women acting thus acquire Dharma, Artha, and Kama, obtain a high position, and generally keep their husbands devoted to them.

[1] This probably refers to a girl married in her infancy, or when very young, whose husband had died before she arrived at the age of puberty.

## Chapter II

*On the Conduct of the Elder Wife Toward the Other Wives of Her Husband, and on That of a Younger Wife Toward the Elder Ones. On the Conduct of a Virgin Widow Remarried. On a Wife Disliked by Her Husband. On the Women in the King's Harem. And, Lastly, on the Conduct of a Husband Toward Many Wives*

The causes of remarriage during the lifetime of the wife are as follows:

1. The folly or ill temper of the wife
2. Her husband's dislike to her
3. The want of offspring
4. The continual birth of daughters
5. The incontinence of the husband

From the very beginning a wife should endeavor to attract the heart of her husband by showing to him continually her devotion, her good temper, and her wisdom. If, however, she bears him no children, she should herself tell her husband to marry another woman. And when the second wife is married, and brought to the house, the first wife should give her a position superior to her own, and look upon her as a sister. In the morning the elder wife should forcibly make the younger one decorate herself in the presence of their husband, and should not mind all the husband's favor being given to her. If the younger wife does anything to displease her husband, the elder one should not neglect her, but should always be ready to give her most careful advice, and should teach her to do various things in the presence of her husband. Her children she should treat as her own, her attendants she should look upon with more regard even than on her own servants, her friends she should cherish with love and kindness, and her relatives with great honor.

When there are many other wives besides herself, the elder wife should associate with the one who is immediately next to her in rank and age, and should instigate the wife who has recently enjoyed her husband's favor to quarrel with the present favorite. After this, she should sympathize with the former, and having collected all the other wives together, should get them to denounce the favorite as a scheming and wicked woman, without, however, committing herself in any way. If the favorite wife happens to quarrel with the husband, then the elder wife should take her part and give her false encouragement, and thus cause the quarrel to be increased. If there be only a little quarrel between the two, the elder wife should do all she can to work it up into a large quarrel. But if after all this she finds that her husband still continues to love his favorite wife, she should then change her tactics, and endeavor to bring about a reconciliation between them, so as to avoid her husband's displeasure.

Thus ends discourse on the conduct of the elder wife.

The younger wife should regard the elder wife of her husband as her mother, and should not give anything away, even to her own relations, without her knowledge. She should tell her everything about herself, and not approach her husband without her permission. Whatever is told to her by the elder wife she should not reveal to others, and she should take care of the children of the senior even more than of her own. When alone with her husband she should serve him well, but should not tell him of the pain she suffers from the existence of a rival wife. She may also obtain secretly from her husband some marks of his particular regard for her, and may tell him that she lives only for him and for the regard that he has for her. She should never reveal her love for her husband, or her husband's love for her to any person, either in pride or in anger, for a wife that reveals the secrets of her husband is despised by him. As for seeking to obtain the regard of her husband, Gonardiya says that it should always be done in private, for fear of the elder wife. If the elder wife be disliked by her husband, or be childless, she should sympathize with her, and should ask her husband to do the same, but should surpass her in leading the life of a chaste woman.

Thus ends discourse on the conduct of the younger wife toward the elder.

A widow in poor circumstances, or of a weak nature, who allies herself again to a man, is called a widow remarried.

The followers of Babhravya say that a virgin widow should not marry a person whom she may be obliged to leave because of his bad character, or of his being destitute of the excellent qualities of a man, or of his being obliged to have recourse to another person. Gonardiya is of opinion that as the cause of a widow's marrying again is her desire for happiness, and as happiness is secured by the possession of excellent qualities in her husband, joined to a love of enjoyment, it is therefore better to secure a person endowed with such qualities in the first instance. Vatsyayana, however, thinks that a widow may marry any person that she likes and that she thinks will suit her.

At the time of her marriage the widow should obtain from her husband the money to pay the cost of drinking parties, and picnics with her relations, and of giving them and her friends kindly gifts and presents; or she may do these things at her own cost if she likes. In the same way she may wear either her husband's ornaments or her own. As to the presents of affection mutually exchanged between the husband and herself, there is no fixed rule about them. If she leaves her husband after marriage of her own accord, she should restore to him whatever he may have given her, with the exception of the mutual presents. If, however, she is driven out of the house by her husband she should not return anything to him.

After her marriage she should live in the house of her husband like one of the chief members of the family, but should treat the other ladies of the family with kindness, the servants with generosity, and all the friends of the house with familiarity and good temper. She should show that she is better acquainted with the sixty-four arts than the other ladies of the house, and in any quarrels with her husband she should not rebuke him severely, but in private do everything that he wishes, and make use of the sixty-four ways of enjoyment. She should be obliging to the other wives of her husband; and to their children she should give presents, behave as their mistress, and make ornaments and playthings for their use. In the friends and servants of her husband she should confide more than in his other wives, and finally she should have a liking for drinking parties, going to picnics, attending fairs and festivals, and for carrying out all kinds of games and amusements.

Thus ends discourse on the conduct of a virgin widow remarried.

A woman who is disliked by her husband, and annoyed and distressed by his other wives, should associate with the wife who is liked most by her husband and who serves him more than the others, and should teach her all the arts with which she is acquainted. She should act as the nurse of her husband's children, and having gained over his friends to her side, should through them make him acquainted of her devotion to him. She should be a leader in religious ceremonies and in vows and fasts, and should not hold too good an opinion of herself. When her husband is lying on his bed, she should go near him only when it is agreeable to him, and should never rebuke him, or show obstinacy in any way. If her husband happens to quarrel with any of his other wives, she should reconcile them to each other, and if he desires to see any woman secretly, she should manage to bring about the meeting between them. She should, moreover, make herself acquainted with the weak points of her husband's character, but always keep them secret, and on the whole behave herself in such a way as may lead him to look upon her as a good and devoted wife.

Here ends discourse on the conduct of a wife disliked by her husband.

The above sections will show how all the women of the king's seraglio are to behave, and therefore we shall now speak separately only about the king.

The female attendants in the harem (called severally Kanchukiyas,[1] Mahallarikas,[2] and Mahallikas[3]), should bring flowers, ointments, and clothes from the king's wives to the king; and he, having received these things, should give them as presents to the servants, along with the things worn by him the previous day. In the afternoon the king, having dressed and put on his ornaments, should interview the women of the harem, who should also be dressed and decorated with jewels. Then, having given to each of them such place and such respect as may suit the occasion and as they may deserve, he should carry on a cheerful conversation with them. After that, he should see such of his wives as may be virgin widows remarried, and after them the concubines and dancing girls. All these should be visited in their own private rooms.

When the king rises from his noonday sleep, the woman

---

[1] A name given to the maidservants of the zenana of the king in ancient times, because they always kept their breasts covered with a cloth called Kanchuki. It was customary in the old time for the maidservants to cover their breasts with a cloth, while the queens kept their breasts uncovered. This custom is distinctly to be seen in the Ajanta cave paintings.

[2] The meaning of this word is "superior woman," so it would seem that a Mahallarika must be a person in authority over the maidservants of the harem.

[3] This was also appertaining to the rank of women employed in the harem. In later times this place was given to eunuchs.

whose duty it is to inform the king regarding the wife who is to spend the night with him should come to him accompanied by the female attendants of that wife whose turn may have arrived in the regular course, and of her who may have been accidentally passed over as her turn arrived, and of her who may have been unwell at the time of her turn. These attendants should place before the king the ointments and unguents sent by each of these wives, marked with the seal of her ring; and their names and their reasons for sending the ointments should be told to the king. After this the king accepts the ointment of one of them, who then is informed that her ointment has been accepted and that her day has been settled.[4]

At festivals, singing parties, and exhibitions all the wives of the king should be treated with respect and served with drinks.

But the women of the harem should not be allowed to go out alone, nor should any women outside the harem be allowed to enter in except those whose character is well known. And, lastly, the work which the king's wives have to do should not be too fatiguing.

Thus ends discourse of the conduct of the king toward the women of the harem, and of their own conduct.

A man marrying many wives should act fairly toward them all. He should neither disregard nor pass over their faults, and should not reveal to one wife the love, passion, bodily blemishes, and confidential reproaches of the other. No opportunity should be given to any one of them of speaking to him about their rivals, and if one of them should begin to speak ill of another, he should chide her and tell her that she

[4] As kings generally had many wives, it was usual for them to enjoy their wives by turns. But as it happened sometimes that some of them lost their turns owing to the king's absence, or to their being unwell, then in such cases the women whose turn had been passed over, and those whose turns had come, used to have a sort of lottery, and the ointment of all the claimants were sent to the king, who accepted the ointment of one of them, and thus settled the question.

has exactly the same blemishes in her character. One of them he should please by secret confidence, another by secret respect, and another by secret flattery, and he should please them all by goings to gardens, by amusements, by presents, by honoring their relations, by telling them secrets, and lastly by loving unions. A young woman who is of a good temper and who conducts herself according to the precepts of the Holy Writ (Dharma Shastras) wins her husband's attachment, and obtains a superiority over her rivals.

Thus ends discourse of the conduct of a husband toward many wives.

# PART FIVE

*About the Wives of Other Men*

## Chapter 1

*On the Characteristics of Men and Women. On the Reasons Why Women Reject the Addresses of Men. On Men Who Have Success With Women; and on Women Who Are Easily Gained Over*

The wives of other people may be resorted to on the occasions already described in Part One, Chapter V, of this work, but the possibility of their acquisition, their fitness for cohabitation, the danger to oneself in uniting with them, and the future effect of these unions, should first of all be examined. A man may resort to the wife of another, for the purpose of saving his own life, when he perceives that his love for her proceeds from one degree of intensity to another. These degrees are ten in number, and are distinguished by the following marks:

1. Love of the eye
2. Attachment of the mind
3. Constant reflection
4. Destruction of sleep
5. Emaciation of the body
6. Turning away from objects of enjoyment
7. Removal of shame
8. Madness
9. Fainting
10. Death

Ancient authors say that a man should know the disposition, truthfulness, purity, and will of a young woman, as also the intensity or weakness of her passions from the form of her body, and from her characteristic marks and signs. But Vatsyayana is of opinion that the forms of bodies and the characteristic marks or signs are but erring tests of character and that women should be judged by their conduct, by the outward expression of their thoughts, and by the movements of their bodies.

Now, as a general rule Gonikaputra says that a woman falls in love with every handsome man she sees, and so does every man at the sight of a beautiful woman, but frequently they do not take any further steps owing to various considerations. In love the following circumstances are peculiar to the woman. She loves without regard to right or wrong and does not try to gain over a man simply for the attainment of some particular purpose. Moreover, when a man first makes up to her she naturally shrinks from him, even though she may be willing to unite herself with him. But when the attempts to gain her are repeated and renewed, she at last consents. But with a man, even though he may have begun to love, he conquers his feelings from a regard for morality and wisdom, and although his thoughts are often on the woman, he does not yield, even though an attempt be made to gain him over. He sometimes makes an attempt or effort to win the object of his affections, and having failed, he leaves her alone for the future. In the same way, once a woman is gained, he often becomes indifferent about her. As for the saying that a man does not care for what is easily gained, and desires only a thing which cannot be obtained without difficulty, it is only a matter of talk.

The causes of a woman rejecting the addresses of a man are as follows:

1. Affection for her husband
2. Desire of lawful progeny
3. Want of opportunity
4. Anger at being addressed by the man too familiarly
5. Difference in rank of life

6. Want of certainty because of the man being devoted to traveling

7. Thinking that the man may be attached to some other person

8. Fear of the man's not keeping his intentions secret

9. Thinking that the man is too devoted to his friends, and has too great a regard for them

10. The apprehension that he is not in earnest

11. Bashfulness because of his being an illustrious man

12. Fear because of his being powerful, or possessed of too impetuous passion, in the case of the deer woman

13. Bashfulness because of his being too clever

14. The thought of having once lived with him on friendly terms only

15. Contempt of his want of knowledge of the world

16. Distrust of his low character

17. Disgust at his want of perception of her love for him

18. In the case of an elephant woman, the thought that he is a hare man, or a man of weak passion

19. Compassion lest any thing befall him because of his passion

20. Despair at her own imperfections

21. Fear of discovery

22. Disillusion at seeing his gray hair or shabby appearance

23. Fear that he may be employed by her husband to test her chastity

24. The thought that he has too much regard for morality

Whichever of the above causes a man may detect, he should endeavor to remove it from the very beginning. Thus, the bashfulness that may arise from his greatness or his ability he should remove by showing his great love and affection for her. The difficulty of the want of opportunity, or of his inaccessibility, he should remove by showing her some easy way of access. The excessive respect entertained by the woman for him should be removed by making himself very familiar. The difficulties that arise from his being thought a low character he should remove by showing his valor and his wisdom; those that come from neglect by extra attention, and those that arise from fear by giving her proper encouragement.

The following are the men who generally obtain success with women:

1. Men well versed in the science of love
2. Men skilled in telling stories
3. Men acquainted with women from their childhood
4. Men who have secured their confidence
5. Men who send presents to them
6. Men who talk well
7. Men who do things that they like
8. Men who have not loved other women previously
9. Men who act as messengers
10. Men who know their weak points
11. Men who are desired by good women
12. Men who are united with their female friends
13. Men who are good looking
14. Men who have been brought up with them
15. Men who are their neighbors
16. Men who are devoted to sexual pleasures, even though these be their own servants
17. The lovers of the daughters of their nurse
18. Men who have been lately married
19. Men who like picnics and pleasure parties
20. Men who are liberal
21. Men who are celebrated for being very strong (bull men)
22. Enterprising and brave men
23. Men who surpass their husbands in learning and good looks, in good qualities, and in liberality
24. Men whose dress and manner of living are magnificent

The following are the women who are easily gained over:

1. Women who stand at the door of their houses
2. Women who are always looking out on the street
3. Women who sit conversing in their neighbor's house
4. A woman who is always staring at you
5. A female messenger
6. A woman who looks sideways at you
7. A woman whose husband has taken another wife without any just cause
8. A woman who hates her husband, or who is hated by him
9. A woman who has nobody to look after her, or keep her in check
10. A woman who has not had any children
11. A woman whose family or caste is not well known
12. A woman whose children are dead
13. A woman who is very fond of society
14. A woman who is apparently very affectionate with her husband
15. The wife of an actor
16. A widow
17. A poor woman
18. A woman fond of enjoyments
19. The wife of a man with many younger brothers
20. A vain woman
21. A woman whose husband is inferior to her in rank or abilities
22. A woman who is proud of her skill in the arts
23. A woman disturbed in mind by the folly of her husband
24. A woman who has been married in her infancy to a rich man, and not liking him when she grows up, desires a man possessing a disposition, talents, and wisdom suitable to her own tastes
25. A woman who is slighted by her husband without any cause
26. A woman who is not respected by other women of the same rank or beauty as herself

27. A woman whose husband is devoted to traveling
28. The wife of a jeweler
29. A jealous woman
30. A covetous woman
31. An immoral woman
32. A barren woman
33. A lazy woman
34. A cowardly woman
35. A humpbacked woman
36. A dwarfish woman
37. A deformed woman
38. A vulgar woman
39. An ill-smelling woman
40. A sick woman
41. An old woman

There are also two verses on the subject, as follows:

"Desire, which springs from nature, and which is increased by art, and from which all danger is taken away by wisdom, becomes firm and secure. A clever man, depending on his own ability, and observing carefully the ideas and thoughts of women, and removing the causes of their turning away from men, is generally successful with them."

## Chapter II

### On Making Acquaintance With the Woman, and on Efforts to Gain Her Over

Ancient authors are of opinion that girls are not so easily seduced by employing female messengers as by the efforts of the man himself but that the wives of others are more easily got at by the aid of female messengers than by the personal efforts of the man. But Vatsyayana lays it down that whenever it is possible a man should always act himself in these matters, and it is only when such is impracticable, or impossible, that female messengers should be employed. As for the saying that women who act and talk boldly and freely are to be won by the personal efforts of the man and that women who do not possess those qualities are to be got at by female messengers, it is only a matter of talk.

Now, when a man himself acts in the matter he should first of all make the acquaintance of the woman he loves in the following manner:

First, he should arrange to be seen by the woman either on a natural or on a special opportunity. A natural opportunity is when one of them goes to the house of the other, and a special opportunity is when they meet either at the house of a friend, or a caste-fellow, or a minister, or a physician, as well as on the occasion of marriage, ceremonies, sacrifices, festivals, funerals, and garden parties.

Second, whenever they do meet, the man should be careful to look at her in such a way as to cause the state of his mind to be known to her; he should pull about his moustache, make a sound with his nails, cause his own ornaments to tinkle, bite his lower lip, and make various other signs of that description. When she is looking at him he should speak to his friends about her and other women, and should show to her his liberality and his appreciation of enjoyments. When sitting by the side of a female friend he should yawn and twist his body, contract his eyebrows, speak very slowly as if he were weary, and listen to her indifferently. A conversation having two meanings should also be carried on with a child or some other person, apparently having regard to a third person, but really having reference to the woman he loves, and this way his love should be made manifest under the pretext of referring to others rather than to herself. He should make marks that have reference to her, on the earth with his nails, or which a stick, and should embrace and kiss a child in her presence, and give it the mixture of betel nut and betel leaves with his tongue, and press its chin with his fingers in a caressing way. All these things should be done at the proper time and in proper places.

Third, the man should fondle a child that may be sitting on her lap, and give it something to play with, and also take the same back again. Conversation with respect to the child may also be held with her, and in this manner he should gradually become well acquainted with her, and he should also make himself agreeable to her relations. Afterward, this acquaintance should be made a pretext for visiting her house frequently, and on such occasions he should converse on the subject of love in her absence, but within her hearing. As his intimacy with her increases, he should place in her charge some kind of deposit or trust, and take away from it a small portion at a time; or he may give her some fragrant substances, or betel nuts to be kept for him by her. After this, he should endeavor to make her well acquainted with his own wife, and get them to carry on confidential conversations, and to sit together in lonely places. In order to see her frequently he should arrange that the same goldsmith, the same jeweler, the same basket maker, the same dyer, and the same washerman be employed by the two families. And he should also pay her long visits openly under the pretense of being engaged with her on business, and one business should lead to another, so as to keep up the intercourse between them. Whenever she wants anything, or is in need of money, or wishes to acquire skill in one of the arts, he should cause her to understand that he is willing and able to do anything that she wants, to give her money, or teach her one of the arts, all these things being quite within his ability and power. In the same way he should hold discussions with her in company with other people, and they should talk of the doings and sayings of other persons, and examine different things like jewelry, precious stones, and so forth. On such occasions he should show her certain things with the values of which she may be unacquainted, and if she begins to dispute with him about the things or their value, he should not contradict her, but point out that he agrees with her in every way.

Thus ends discourse of the ways of making the acquaintance of the woman desired.

Now, after a girl has become acquainted with the man as above described, and has manifested her love to him by the various outward signs and by the motions of her body, the man should make every effort to gain her over. But as girls are not acquainted with sexual union, they should be treated with the greatest delicacy, and the man should proceed with considerable caution, though in the case of other women accustomed to sexual intercourse this is not necessary. When the intentions of the girl are known, and her bashfulness put aside, the man should begin to make use of her money, and an interchange of clothes, rings, and flowers should be made. In this, the man should take particular care that the things given by him are handsome and valuable. He should, moreover, receive from her a mixture of betel leaves, and when he is going to a party he should ask for the flower in her hair or the flower in her hand. If he himself gives her a flower, it should be a sweet-smelling one, marked with marks made by his nails or teeth. With increasing assiduity he should dispel her fears, and by degrees get her to go with him to some lonely place, and there he should embrace and kiss her. And finally, at the time of giving her some betel nut, or of receiving the same from her, or at the time of making an exchange of flowers, he should touch and press her private parts, thus bringing his efforts to a satisfactory conclusion.

When a man is endeavoring to seduce one woman, he should not attempt to seduce any other at the same time. But after he has succeeded with the first, and enjoyed her for a considerable time, he can keep her affections by giving her presents that she likes, and then commence making up to another woman. When a man sees the husband of a woman going to some place near his house, he should not enjoy the woman then, even though she may be easily gained over at that time. A wise man, having a regard for his reputation, should not think of seducing a woman who is apprehensive, timid, or not to be trusted, or one who is well guarded or possessed of a father-in-law or mother-in-law.

## Chapter III

### Examination of the State of a Woman's Mind

When a man is trying to gain over a woman, he should examine the state of her mind, and act as follows.

If she listens to him, but does not manifest to him in any way her own intentions, he should then try to gain her over by means of a go-between.

If she meets him once, and again comes to meet him better dressed than before, or comes to him in some lonely place, he should be certain that she is capable of being enjoyed by the use of a little force. A woman who lets a man make up to her, but does not give herself up, even after a long time, should be considered a trifler in love; but owing to the fickleness of the human mind, even such a woman can be conquered by always keeping up a close acquaintance with her.

When a woman avoids the attentions of a man, and because of respect for him and pride in herself will not meet him or approach him, she can be gained over with difficulty, either by endeavoring to keep on familiar terms with her or else by an exceedingly clever go-between.

When a man makes up to a woman, and she reproaches him with harsh words, she should be abandoned at once.

When a woman reproaches a man, but at the same time acts affectionately toward him, she should be made love to in every way.

A woman who meets a man in lonely places, and puts up with the touch of his foot, but pretends, because of the indecision of her mind, not to be aware of it, should be conquered by patience, and by continued efforts as follows:

If she happens to go to sleep in his vicinity, he should put his left arm around her, and see when she awakes whether she repulses him in reality, or only as if she were desirous of the same thing being done to her again. And what is done by the arm can also be done by the foot. If the man succeeds in this point, he should embrace her more closely; and if she will not stand the embrace, and gets up, but behaves with him as usual the next day, he should consider then that she is not unwilling to be enjoyed by him. If, however, she does not appear again, the man should try to win her over by means of a go-between; and if, after having disappeared for some time she again appears, and behaves with him as usual, the man should then consider that she would not object to being united with him.

When a woman gives a man an opportunity, and makes her own love manifest to him, he should proceed to enjoy her. And the signs of a woman manifesting her love are these:

1. She calls out to a man without being addressed by him in the first instance.

2. She shows herself to him in secret places.

3. She speaks to him tremblingly and inarticulately.

4. The fingers of her hand and the toes of her feet are moistened with perspiration, and her face is blooming with delight.

5. She occupies herself with shampooing his body and pressing his head.

6. When shampooing him, she works with one hand only, and with the other she touches and embraces parts of his body.

7. She remains with both hands placed on his body motionless, as if she had been surprised by something or was overcome by fatigue.

8. She sometimes bends her face down upon his thighs, and when asked to shampoo them does not manifest any unwillingness to do so.

9. She places one of her hands quite motionless on his body, and even though the man should press it between two members of his body, she does not remove it for a long time.

10. Lastly, when she has resisted all the efforts of the man to gain her over, she returns to him the next day to shampoo his body as before.

When a woman neither gives encouragement to a man nor avoids him, but hides herself and remains in some lonely place, she must be got at by means of the female servant who may be near her. If when called by the man she acts in the same way, then she should be gained over by means of a skillful go-between. But if she will have nothing to say to the man, he should consider well before he begins any further attempts to gain her over.

Thus ends the examination of the state of a woman's mind.

A man should first get himself introduced to a woman, and then carry on a conversation with her. He should give her hints of his love for her, and if he finds from her replies that she receives these hints favorably, he should then set to work to gain her over without any fear. A woman who shows her love by outward signs to the man at his first interview should be gained over very easily. In the same way a lascivious woman, who when addressed in loving words replies openly in words expressive of her love, should be considered to have been gained over at that very moment. With regard to all women, whether they be wise, simple, or confiding, this rule is laid down that those who make an open manifestation of their love are easily gained over.

## Chapter IV

### The Business of a Go-Between

If a woman has manifested her love or desire either by signs or by motions of the body, and is afterward rarely or never seen anywhere, or if a woman is met for the first time, the man should get a go-between to approach her.

Now the go-between, having wheedled herself into the confidence of the woman by acting according to her disposition, should try to make her hate or despise her husband by holding artful conversations with her, by telling about medicines for getting children, by talking to her about other people, by tales of various kinds, by stories about the wives of other men, and by praising her beauty, wisdom, generosity, and good nature, and by saying to her: "It is indeed a pity that you, who are so excellent a woman in every way, should be possessed of a husband of this kind. Beautiful lady, he is not fit even to serve you." The go-between should further talk to the woman about the weakness of the passion of her husband, his jealousy, his roguery, his ingratitude, his aversion to enjoyments, his dullness, his meanness, and all the other faults that he may have, and with which she may be acquainted. She should particularly harp upon that fault or failing by which the wife may appear to be most affected. If the wife be a deer woman, and the husband a hare man, then there would be no fault in that direction, but in the event of

186

his being a hare man, and she a mare woman or elephant woman, then this fault should be pointed out to her.

Gonikaputra is of the opinion that when it is the first affair of the woman, or when her love has been only very secretly shown, the man should then secure and send to her a go-between with whom she may be already acquainted and in whom she confides.

But to return to our subject. The go-between should tell the woman about the obedience and love of the man, and as her confidence and affection increase, she should then explain to her the thing to be accomplished in the following way: "Hear this, O beautiful lady. This man, born of a good family, having seen you, has gone mad on your account. The poor young man, who is tender by nature, has never been distressed in such a way before, and it is highly probable that he will succumb under his present affliction, and experience the pains of death." If the woman listens with a favorable ear, then on the following day the go-between, having observed marks of good spirits in her face, in her eyes, and in her manner of conversation, should again converse with her on the subject of the man, and should tell her the stories of Ahalya [1] and Indra, of Shakuntala [2] and Dushyanti, and such others as may be fit for the occasion. She should also describe to her the strength of the man, his talents, his skill in the sixty-four sorts of enjoyments mentioned by Babhravya, his good looks, and his liaison with some praiseworthy woman, no matter whether this last ever took place or not.

In addition to this, the go-between should carefully note the behavior of the woman, which if favorable would be as follows: She would address her with a smiling look, would

[1] The wife of the sage Gautama; she was seduced by Indra the king of the gods.

[2] The heroine of one of the best, if not the best, of Hindu plays, and the best known in Sanskrit dramatic literature. It was first brought to notice by Sir William Jones, and has been well and poetically translated by Arthur W. Ryder in a volume entitled *Shakuntala and Other Writings* by Kalidasa (Dutton Paperbacks, D40).

seat herself close beside her, and ask her, "Where have you been? What have you been doing? Where did you dine? Where did you sleep? Where have you been sitting?" Moreover, the woman would meet the go-between in lonely places and tell her stories there, would yawn contemplatively, draw long sighs, give her presents, remember her on occasions of festivities, dismiss her with a wish to see her again, and say to her jestingly, "O well-speaking woman, why do you speak these bad words to me?" She would discourse on the sin of her union with the man, would not tell her about any previous visits or conversations that she may have had with him, but would wish to be asked about these, and lastly would laugh at the man's desire, but would not reproach him in any way.

Thus ends the behavior of the woman with the go-between.

When the woman manifests her love in the manner above described, the go-between should increase it by bringing to her love tokens from the man. But if the woman be not acquainted with the man personally, the go-between should win her over by extolling and praising his good qualities, and by telling stories about his love for her. Here Auddalaka says that when a man and woman are not personally acquainted with each other, and have not shown each other any signs of affection, the employment of a go-between is useless.

The followers of Babhravya, on the other hand, affirm that even though they be personally unacquainted, but have shown each other signs of affection, there is an occasion for the employment of a go-between. Gonikaputra asserts that a go-between should be employed, provided they are acquainted with each other, even though no signs of affection may have passed between them. Vatsyayana, however, lays it down that even though they may not be personally acquainted with each other, and may not have shown each other any signs of affection, still they are both capable of placing confidence in a go-between.

Now the go-between should show to the woman the presents, such as the betel nut and the betel leaves, the perfumes, the flowers, and the rings the man may have given to her for the sake of the woman, and on these presents should be impressed the marks of the man's teeth and nails, and other signs. On the cloth that he may send he should draw with saffron both his hands joined together as if in earnest entreaty.

The go-between should also show to the woman ornamental figures of various kinds cut in leaves, together with ear ornaments, and chaplets made of flowers containing love letters expressive of the desire of the man, and she should cause her to send affectionate presents to the man in return. After they have mutually accepted each other's presents, a meeting should be arranged between them on the faith of the go-between.

The followers of Babhravya say that this meeting should take place at the time of going to the temple of a deity; or on occasions of fairs, garden parties, theatrical performances, marriages, sacrifices, festivals, and funerals, as well as at the time of going to the river to bathe, or at times of natural calamities,[3] during fear of robbers or of hostile invasions of the country.

Gonikaputra is of the opinion, however, that these meetings had better be brought about in the abodes of female friends, mendicants, astrologers, and ascetics. But Vatsyayana decides that only that place is well suited for the purpose which has proper means of ingress and egress, and where arrangements have been made to prevent any accidental occurrence, and where a man who has once entered the house can also leave it at the proper time without any disagreeable encounter.

Now, go-betweens or female messengers are of the following different kinds:

1. A go-between who takes upon herself the whole burden of the business.

2. A go-between who does only a limited part of the business.

[3] It is supposed that storms, earthquakes, famines, and pestilent diseases are here alluded to.

3. A go-between who is the bearer of a letter only.
4. A go-between acting on her own account.
5. The go-between of an innocent young woman.
6. A wife serving as a go-between.
7. A mute go-between.
8. A go-between who acts the part of the wind.

(1). A woman who, having observed the mutual passion of a man and woman, brings them together and arranges it by the power of her own intellect, such a one is called a go-between who takes upon herself the whole burden of the business. This kind of go-between is chiefly employed when the man and the woman are already acquainted with each other, and have conversed together, and in such cases she is sent not only by the man (as is always done in all other cases) but by the woman also. The above name is also given to a go-between who, perceiving that the man and the woman are suited to each other, tries to bring about a union between them even though they are not acquainted with each other.

(2). A go-between who, perceiving that some part of the affair is already done, or that the advances on the part of the man are already made, completes the rest of the business is called a go-between who performs only a limited part of the business.

(3). A go-between who simply carries messages between a man and a woman who love each other but who cannot frequently meet is called the bearer of a letter or message.

This name is also given to one who is sent by either of the lovers to acquaint either the one or the other with the time and place of their meeting.

(4). A woman who goes herself to a man, and tells him of her having enjoyed sexual union with him in a dream, and expresses her anger at his wife having rebuked him for calling her by the name of her rival instead of by her own name, and gives him something bearing the marks of her teeth and nails, and informs him that she knew she was formerly desired by him, and asks him privately whether she or his wife is the better looking, such a person is called a woman who is a go-between for herself. Now, such a woman should be met and interviewed by the man in private and secretly.

The above name is also given to a woman who, having made an agreement with some other woman to act as her go-between, gains the man for herself by making him personally acquainted with herself, and thus causes the other woman to fail. The same applies to a man who, acting as a go-between for another, and having no previous connection with the woman, gains her for himself, and thus causes the failure of the other man.

(5). A woman who has gained the confidence of the innocent young wife of any man, and who has learned her secrets without exercising any pressure on her mind, and found out from her how her husband behaves to her, if this woman then teaches her the art of securing his favor, and decorates her so as to show her love, and instructs her how and when to be angry, or to pretend to be so, and then, having herself made marks of the nails and teeth on the body of the wife, gets the latter to send for her husband to show these marks to him, and thus excite him for enjoyment, such is called the go-between of an innocent young woman. In such cases the man should send replies to his wife through the same woman.

(6). When a man gets his wife to gain the confidence of a woman whom he wants to enjoy, and to call on her and talk to her about the wisdom and ability of her husband, that wife is called a wife serving as a go-between. In this case the feelings of the woman with regard to the man should also be made known through the wife.

(7). When any man sends a girl or a female servant to any woman under some pretext or other, and places a letter in her bouquet of flowers, or in her ear ornaments, or marks something about her with his teeth or nails, that girl or female servant is called a mute go-between. In this case the man should expect an answer from the woman through the same person.

(8). A person who carries a message to a woman which has a double meaning, or which relates to some past transactions, or which is unintelligible to other people, is called a go-between who acts the part of the wind. In this case the reply should be asked for through the same woman.

Thus ends the discourse of the different kinds of go-betweens.

A female astrologer, a female servant, a female beggar, or a female artist are well acquainted with the business of a go-between, and very soon gain the confidence of other women. Any one of them can raise enmity between any two persons if she wishes to do so, or extol the loveliness of any woman that she wishes to praise, or describe the arts practiced by other women in sexual union. They can also speak highly of the love of a man, of his skill in sexual enjoyment, and of the desire of other women, more beautiful even than the woman they are addressing, for him, and explain the restraint under which he may be at home.

Lastly, a go-between can by the artfulness of her conversation unite a woman with a man, even though he may not have been thought of by her, or though she may have been considered beyond his aspirations. She can also bring back a man to a woman who, owing to some cause or other, has separated himself from her.

## Chapter V

### On the Love of Persons in Authority for the Wives of Other Men

Kings and their ministers have no access to the abodes of others; moreover, their mode of living is constantly watched and observed and imitated by the people at large, just as the animal world, seeing the sun rise, get up after him, and when he sets in the evening, lie down again in the same way. Therefore persons in authority should not do any improper act in public, since such are reprehensible for one in their position, and would be deserving of censure. But if they find that such an act is necessary to be done, they should make use of the proper means, as described in the following paragraphs.

The head man of the Village (Gramani), the king's officer employed there, and the man [1] whose business it is to glean corn, can gain over female villagers simply by asking them. It is on this account that this class of woman are called unchaste women by voluptuaries.

The union of the above-mentioned men with this class of woman takes place on the occasions of unpaid labor, of filling the granaries in their houses, of taking things in and out of the house, of cleaning the houses, of working in the fields, and of purchasing cotton, wool, flax, hemp, and thread, and at the season of the purchase, sale, and exchange of various other articles, as well as at the time of doing various other

[1] This is a phrase used for the man who does the work of everybody, and who is fed by the whole village.

works. In the same way the superintendents of cow pens enjoy the women in the cow pens; and officers who have the superintendence of widows, of women who are without supporters, and of women who have left their husbands have sexual intercourse with these women. The intelligent accomplish their object by wandering at night in the village, while villagers also unite with the wives of their sons, being much alone with them. Lastly, the superintendents of markets have a great deal to do with female villagers at the time of their making purchases in the market.

(1). During the festival of the eighth moon, that is, during the bright half of the month of Nargashirsha, as also during the moonlight festival of the month of Kartika, and the spring festival of Chaitra, the women of cities and towns generally visit the women of the king's harem in the royal palace. These visitors go to the several apartments of the women of the harem, as they are acquainted with them, and pass the night in conversation, and in proper sports and amusement, and go away in the morning. On such occasions a female attendant of the king (previously acquainted with the woman whom the king desires), should loiter about, and accost this woman when she sets out to go home, and induce her to come and see the amusing things in the palace. Even before these festivals, the attendant should have caused it to be intimated to this woman that on the occasion of this festival she would show her all the interesting things in the royal palace. Accordingly she should show her the bower of the coral creeper, the garden house with its floor inlaid with precious stones, the bower of grapes, the building on the water, the secret passages in the walls of the palace, the pictures, the sporting animals, the machines, the birds, and the cages of the lions and the tigers. After this, when alone with her, she should tell her about the love of the king for her, and should describe to her the good fortune which would attend upon her union with the king, giving her at the time a strict promise of secrecy. If the woman does not accept the offer, the attendant should conciliate and please her with handsome presents befitting the position of the king, and having accompanied her for some distance should dismiss her with great affection.

(2). Or, having made the acquaintance of the husband of the woman whom the king desires, the wives of the king should get the wife to pay them a visit in the harem, and on this occasion a female attendant of the king, having been sent thither, should act as described above.

(3). Or one of the king's wives should get acquainted with the woman that the king desires, by sending one of the female attendants to her, who should, on their becoming more intimate, induce her to come and see the royal abode. Afterward, when she has visited the harem, and acquired confidence, a female confidante of the king, sent thither, should act as before described.

(4). Or the king's wife should invite the woman whom the king desires, to come to the royal palace, so that she might see the practice of the art in which the king's wife may be skilled, and after she has come to the harem, a female attendant of the king, sent thither, should act as before described.

(5). Or a female beggar, in league with the king's wife, should say to the woman desired by the king, and whose husband may have lost his wealth, or may have some cause for fear from the king: "This wife of the king has influence over him; she is, moreover, naturally kindhearted, and we must therefore go to her in this matter. I shall arrange for your entrance into the harem, and she will do away with all cause of danger and fear from the king." If the woman accepts this offer, the female beggar should take her two or three times to the harem, and the king's wife there should give her a promise of protection. After this, when the woman, delighted with her reception and promise of protection, again goes to the harem, then a female attendant of the king, sent thither, should act as directed.

(6). What has been said above regarding the wife of one

who has some cause for fear from the king applies also to the wives of those who seek service under the king or who are oppressed by the king's ministers, or who are poor, or who are not satisfied with their position, or who are desirous of gaining the king's favor, or who wish to become famous among the people, or who are oppressed by the members of their own caste or who want to injure their caste fellows, or who are spies of the king, or who have any other object to attain.

(7). Lastly, if the woman desired by the king be living with some person who is not her husband, then the king should cause her to be arrested, and having made her a slave because of her crime, should place her in the harem. Or the king should cause his ambassador to quarrel with the husband of the woman desired by him, and should then imprison her as the wife of an enemy of the king, and by this means should place her in the harem.

Thus ends discourse of the means of gaining over the wives of others secretly.

The above-mentioned ways of gaining over the wives of other men are chiefly practiced in the palaces of kings. But a king should never enter the abode of another person, for Abhira [2] the King of the Kottas was killed by a washerman while in the house of another, and in the same way Jayasana the King of the Kashis was slain by the commandant of his cavalry (Senapati).

But according to the customs of some countries, there are facilities for kings to make love to the wives of other men. Thus in the country of the Andras the newly married daughters of the people thereof enter the king's harem with some presents on the tenth day of their marriage, and having been enjoyed by the king are then to serve him. In the country of the Vaidarbbas the wives of the chief ministers approach the king at night to serve him. In the country of

---

[2] The exact date of the reign of these kings is not known. It is supposed to have been about the beginning of the Christian Era.

the Vaidarbbas the beautiful wives of the inhabitants pass a month in the king's harem under the pretense of affection for the king. In the country of the Aparatakas the people gave their beautiful wives as presents to the ministers and the kings. And lastly, in the country of the Saurashtras the women of the city and the country enter the royal harem for the king's pleasure either together or separately.

There are also two verses on the subject, as follows:

"The above and other ways are the means employed in different countries by kings with regards to the wives of other persons. But a king who has the welfare of his people at heart should not on any account put them into practice."

"A king who has conquered the six [3] enemies of mankind becomes the master of the whole earth."

[3] These are Lust, Anger, Avarice, Spiritual Ignorance, Pride, and Envy.

## Chapter VI

### About the Women of the Royal Harem; and on the Keeping of One's Own Wife

The women of the royal harem cannot see or meet any men because of their being strictly guarded, neither do they have their desires satisfied, because their only husband is common to many wives. For this reason, among themselves they give pleasure to each other in various ways as now described.

Having dressed the daughters of their nurses, or their female friends, or their female attendants, like men, they accomplish their object by means of bulbs, roots, and fruits having the form of the lingam, or they lie down upon the statue of a male figure, in which the lingam is visible and erect.

Some kings, who are compassionate, take or apply certain medicines to enable them to enjoy many wives in one night, simply for the purpose of satisfying the desire of their women, though they perhaps have no desire of their own. Others enjoy with great affection only those wives that they particularly like, while others take them only as the turn of each wife arrives, in due course. Such are the ways of enjoyment prevalent in Eastern countries, and what is said about the means of enjoyment of the female is also applicable to the male.

By means of their female attendants the ladies of the royal harem generally get men into their apartments in the disguise or dress of women. Their female attendants, and the daughters of their nurses, who are acquainted with their secrets, should exert themselves to get men to come to the harem in this way by telling them of the good fortune attending it, and by describing the facilities of entering and leaving the palace, the large size of the premises, the carelessness of the sentinels, and the irregularities of the attendants about the persons of the royal wives. But these women should never induce a man to enter the harem by telling him falsehoods, for that would probably lead to his destruction.

As for the man himself, he had better not enter a royal harem, even though it may be easily accessible, because of the numerous disasters to which he may be exposed there. If, however, he wants to enter it, he should first ascertain whether there is an easy way to get out, whether it is closely surrounded by the pleasure garden, whether it has separate enclosures belonging to it, whether the sentinels are careless, whether the king has gone abroad, and then, when he is called by the women of the harem, he should carefully observe the localities, and enter by the way pointed out by them. If he is able to manage it, he should hang about the harem every day, and, under some pretext or other, make friends with the sentinels, and show himself attached to the female attendants of the harem, who may have become acquainted with his design, and to whom he should express his regret at not being able to obtain the object of his desire. Lastly, he should cause the whole business of a go-between to be done by the woman who may have access to the harem, and he should be careful to be able to recognize the emissaries of the king.

When a go-between has no access to the harem, then the man should stand in some place where the lady whom he loves and whom he is anxious to enjoy can be seen.

If that place is occupied by the king's sentinels, he should then disguise himself as a female attendant of the lady who comes to the place, or passes by it. When she looks at him he should let her know his feeling by outward signs and gestures, and should show her pictures, things with double meanings, chaplets of flowers, and rings. He should carefully mark the answer she gives, whether by word or by sign or by gesture, and should then try and get into the harem. If he is certain of her coming to some particular place, he should conceal himself there, and at the appointed time should enter along with her as one of the guards. He may also go in and out, concealed in a folded bed, or bed covering, or with his body made invisible,[1] by means of external applications, a recipe for one of which is as follows:

The heart of an ichneumon, the fruit of the long gourd (Tumbaki), and the eyes of a serpent should all be burned without letting out the smoke; the ashes should then be ground and mixed in equal quantities with water. By putting this mixture upon the eyes a man can go about unseen.

Other means of invisibility are prescribed by Dhyana Brahmans and Yogashiras.

Again, the man may enter the harem during the festival of the eighth moon in the month of Nargashirsha, and during the moonlight festivals when the female attendants of the harem are all busily occupied, or in confusion.

The following principles are laid down on this subject:

The entrance of young men into harems, and their exit from them, generally take place when things are being brought into the palace, or when things are being taken out of it, or when drinking festivals are going on, or when the female attendants are in a hurry, or when the residence of some of the royal ladies is being changed, or when the king's wives go to gardens or to fairs, or when they enter the palace on their return from them, or lastly, when the king is absent on a long pilgrimage. The women of the royal harem know each other's secrets, and having but one object to attain, they give assistance to each other. A young man who enjoys all

[1] The way to make oneself invisible; the knowledge of the art of transmigration, or changing ourselves or others into any shape or form by the use of charms and spells; the power of being in two places at once; and other occult sciences are frequently referred to in Oriental literatures.

of them, and who is common to them all, can continue enjoying his union with them so long as it is kept quiet, and is
not known abroad.

Now, in the country of the Aparatikas the royal ladies are
not well protected, and consequently many young men are
passed into the harem by the women who have access to the
royal palace. The wives of the king of the Abhira country accomplish their objects with those sentinels in the harem who
bear the name of Kshatriyas. The royal ladies in the country
of the Vatsagulmas cause such men as are suitable to enter
into the harem along with their female messengers. In the
country of the Vaidarbhas the sons of the royal ladies enter
the royal harem when they please, and enjoy the women, with
the exception of their own mothers. In the Stri Rajya the wives
of the king are enjoyed by his caste fellows and relations. In
the Gandak country the royal wives are enjoyed by Brahmans,
friends, servants, and slaves. In the Samdhava country, servants, foster children, and other persons like them enjoy the
women of the harem. In the country of the Himalayas ad-
venturous citizens bribe the sentinels and the harem. In the
country of the Vanyas and the Kalmyas, Brahmans, with the
knowledge of the king, enter the harem under the pretense
of giving flowers to the ladies, and speak with them from
behind a curtain, and from such conversation union afterward takes place. Lastly, the women in the harem of the
king of the Prachyas conceal one young man in the harem for
every batch of nine or ten of the women.

Thus act the wives of the others.

For these reasons a man should guard his own wife. Old
authors say that a king should select for sentinels in his harem
such men as have had their freedom from carnal desires well
tested. But such men, though free themselves from carnal
desire, by reason of their fear or avarice may cause other
persons to enter the harem, and therefore Gonikaputra says
that kings should place such men in the harem as may have
had their freedom from carnal desires, their fears, and their

avarice well tested. Lastly, Vatsyayana says that under the influence of Dharma [2] people might be admitted, and therefore men should be selected who are free from carnal desires, fear, avarice, and Dharma.

The followers of Babhravya say that a man should cause his wife to associate with a young woman who would tell him the secrets of other people, and thus find out from her about his wife's chastity. But Vatsyayana says that as wicked persons are always successful with women, a man should not cause his innocent wife to be corrupted by bringing her into the company of a deceitful woman.

The following are the causes of the destruction of a woman's chastity:

Always going into society, and sitting in company
Absence of restraint
The loose habits of her husband
Want of caution in her relations with other men
Continued and long absence of her husband
Living in a foreign country
Destruction of her love and feelings by her husband
The company of loose women
The jealousy of her husband

There are also the following verses on the subject:
"A clever man, learning from the Shastras the ways of winning over the wives of other people, is never deceived in the case of his own wives. No one, however, should make use of these ways for seducing the wives of others, because they do not always succeed, and, moveover, often cause disasters, and the destruction of Dharma and Artha. This book, which is intended for the good of people, and to teach them the ways of guarding their own wives, should not be made use of merely for gaining over the wives of others."

[2] This may be considered as meaning religious influence, and alludes to persons who might be gained over by that means.

# PART SIX

*About Courtesans*

———————

## Chapter I

*On the Causes of a Courtesan Resorting to Men;*
*On the Means of Attaching to Herself the Man*
*Desired; and on the Kind of Man That It Is De-*
*sirable to Be Acquainted With*

By having intercourse with men, courtesans obtain sexual pleasure, as well as their own maintenance. Now, when a courtesan takes up with a man from love, the action is natural; but when she resorts to him for the purpose of getting money, her action is artificial or forced. Even in this latter case, however, she should conduct herself as if her love were indeed natural, because men repose their confidence in those women who apparently love them. In making known her love to the man, she should show an entire freedom from avarice, and for the sake of her future credit she should abstain from acquiring money from him by unlawful means.

A courtesan, well dressed and wearing her ornaments, should sit or stand at the door of her house, and without exposing herself too much, should look on the public road so as to be seen by the passersby, she being like an object on view for sale. She should form friendships with such persons as would enable her to separate men from other women, and attach them to herself, to repair her own misfortunes, to acquire wealth, and to protect her from being bullied or set upon by persons with whom she may have dealings of some kind or another.

These persons are:

The guards of the town, or the police
The officers of the courts of justice
Astrologers
Powerful men, or men with interest
Learned men
Teachers of the sixty-four arts
Pithamardas or confidants
Vitas or parasites
Vidushakas or jesters
Flower sellers
Perfumers
Vendors of spirits
Washermen
Barbers
Beggars

And such other persons as may be found necessary for the particular object to be acquired.

The following kinds of men may be taken up with, simply for the purpose of getting their money:

Men of independent income
Young men
Men who are free from any ties
Men who hold places of authority under the king
Men who have secured their means of livelihood without difficulty
Men possessed of unfailing sources of income
Men who consider themselves handsome
Men who are always praising themselves
One who is a eunuch, but wishes to be thought a man
One who hates his equals
One who is naturally liberal
One who has influence with the king or his ministers

One who is always fortunate
One who is proud of his wealth
One who disobeys the orders of his elders
One upon whom the members of his caste keep an eye
An only son whose father is wealthy
An ascetic who is internally troubled with desire
A brave man
A physician of the king
Previous acquaintances

On the other hand, those who are possessed of excellent qualities are also to be resorted to for the sake of love and fame. Such men are as follows:

Men of high birth, learned, with a good knowledge of the world, and doing the proper things at the proper times; poets, good storytellers, eloquent men, energetic men skilled in various arts, farseeing into the future, possessed of great minds, full of perseverance, of a firm devotion, free from anger, liberal, affectionate to their parents, and with a liking for all social gatherings, skilled in completing verses begun by others and in various other sports, free from all disease, possessed of a perfect body, strong, and not addicted to drinking, powerful in sexual enjoyment, sociable, showing love toward woman and attracting their hearts to himself but not entirely devoted to them, possessed of independent means of livelihood, free from envy and, last of all, free from suspicion.

Such are the good qualities of a man.

The woman also should have the following characteristics:

She should be possessed of beauty and amiability, with auspicious body marks. She should have a liking for good qualities in other people, as well as a liking for wealth. She should take delight in sexual unions resulting from love, and should be of firm mind, and of the same class as the man with regard to sexual enjoyment.

She should always be anxious to acquire and obtain experience and knowledge, be free from avarice, and always have a liking for social gatherings, and for the arts.

The following are the ordinary qualities of all women:

To be possessed of intelligence, good disposition, and good manners; to be straightforward in behavior, and to be grateful; to consider well the future before doing anything; to possess activity, to be of consistent behavior, and to have a knowledge of the proper times and places for doing things; to speak always without meanness, loud laughter, malignity, anger, avarice, dullness, or stupidity, to have a knowledge of the *Kama Sutra,* and to be skilled in all the arts connected with it.

The faults of the women are to be known by the absence of any of the above-mentioned good qualities.

The following kinds of men are not fit to be resorted to by courtesans:

One who is consumptive; one who is sickly; one whose mouth contains worms; one whose breath smells like human excrement; one whose wife is dear to him; one who speaks harshly; one who is always suspicious; one who is avaricious; one who is pitiless; one who is a thief; one who is self-conceited; one who has a liking for sorcery; one who does not care for respect or disrespect; one who can be gained over even by his enemies by means of money; and lastly, one who is extremely bashful.

Ancient authors are of the opinion that the causes of a courtesan resorting to men are: love, fear, money, pleasure, returning some act of enmity, curiosity, sorrow, constant intercourse, Dharma, celebrity, compassion, the desire of having a friend, shame, the likeness of the man to some beloved person, the search after good fortune, getting rid of the love of somebody else, being of the same class as the man with respect to sexual union, living in the same place, constancy, and poverty. But Vatsyayana decides that desire of wealth, freedom from misfortune, and love are the only causes that affect the union of courtesans with men.

Now, a courtesan should not sacrifice money to her love, because money is the chief thing to be attended to. But in cases of fear, and so on, she should pay regard to strength and other qualities. Moreover, even though she be invited by any man to join him, she should not at once consent to a union, because men are apt to despise things which are easily acquired. On such occasions she should first send the shampooers and the singers and the jesters who may be in her service, or in their absence the Pithamadras, or confidants, and others, to find out the state of his feelings and the condition of his mind. By means of these persons she should ascertain whether the man is pure or impure, affected or unaffected, capable of attachment, or indifferent, liberal or niggardly; and if she finds him to her liking, she should then employ the Vita and others to attach his mind to her.

Accordingly, the Pithamarda should bring the man to her house, under the pretense of seeing the fights of quails, cocks, and rams, of hearing the myna (a kind of starling) talk, or of seeing some other spectacle, or the practice of some art; or he may take the woman to the abode of the man. After this, when the man comes to her house, the woman should give him something capable of producing curiosity and love in his heart, such as an affectionate present, telling him that it was specially designed for his use. She should also amuse him for a long time by telling him such stories and doing such things as he may take most delight in. When he goes away she should frequently send to him a female attendant, skilled in carrying on a jesting conversation, and also a small present at the same time. She should also sometimes go to him herself under the pretense of some business, and accompanied by the Pithamarda.

Thus ends discourse of the means of attaching to herself the man desired.

There are also some verses on the subject, as follows:

"When a lover comes to her abode, a courtesan should give him a mixture of betel leaves and betel nut, garlands of flowers, and perfumed ointments, and, showing her skill in arts, should entertain him with a long conversation. She should also give him some loving presents, and make an exchange of her own things with him, and at the same time should show him her skill in sexual enjoyment. When a courtesan is thus united with her lover, she should always delight him by affectionate gifts, by conversation, and by the application of tender means of enjoyment."

## Chapter II

### On a Courtesan Living Like a Wife

When a courtesan is living as a wife with her lover, she should behave like a chaste woman, and do everything to his satisfaction. Her duty in this respect, in short, is that she should give him pleasure but should not become attached to him, though behaving as if she were really attached.

Now, the following is the manner in which she is to conduct herself so as to accomplish the above-mentioned purpose. She should have a mother dependent on her, one who is represented as very harsh, and who looks upon money as her chief object in life. If there is no mother, then an old and confidential nurse should play the same role. The mother, or nurse, on her part, should appear to be displeased with the lover, and forcibly take the courtesan away from him. The woman herself should always show pretended anger, dejection, fear, and shame on this account, but should not disobey the mother or nurse at any time.

She should pretend to the mother or nurse that the man is suffering from bad health; and, making this a pretext for going to see him, she should go on that account. She is, moreover, to practice the following things for the purpose of gaining the man's favor:

Sending her female attendant to bring the flowers used by him on the previous day, in order that she may use them herself as a mark of affection; asking for the mixture of betel nut and leaves that have remained uneaten by him; expressing wonder at his knowledge of sexual intercourse, and the several means of enjoyment used by him; learning from him the sixty-four kinds of pleasure mentioned by Babhravya; continually practicing the ways of enjoyment as taught by him and according to his liking; keeping his secrets; telling him her own desires and secrets; concealing her anger; never neglecting him on the bed when he turns his face toward her; touching any parts of his body according to his wish; kissing and embracing him when he is asleep; looking at him with apparent anxiety when he is rapt in thought or thinking of some other subject than herself; showing neither complete shamelessness nor excessive bashfulness when he meets her or sees her standing on the terrace of her house from the public road; hating his enemies; loving those who are dear to him; showing a liking for that which he likes; being in high or low spirits according to the state that he is in himself; expressing a curiosity to see his wives; not continuing her anger for a long time; suspecting even the marks and wounds made by herself with her nails and teeth on his body to have been made by some other woman; keeping her love for him unexpressed by words but showing it by deeds and signs and hints; remaining silent when he is asleep, intoxicated, or sick; being very attentive when he describes his good actions, and reciting them afterward to his praise and benefit; giving witty replies to him if he be sufficiently attached to her; listening to all his stories except those that relate to her rivals; expressing feelings of dejection and sorrow if he sighs, yawns, or falls down; pronouncing the words "live long" when he sneezes; pretending to be ill or to having the desire of pregnancy when he feels dejected; abstaining from praising the good qualities of anybody else and from censuring those who possess the same faults as her own man; wearing anything that may have been given to her by him; abstaining from putting on her ornaments, and from taking food when he is in pain, sick, low-spirited, or suffering from misfortune, and condoling and lamenting with him over the same; wishing to accompany him if he happens to leave the country himself or if he be banished from it by the king; expressing a desire not to live after him; telling him that the whole object and desire of her life was to be united with him; offering previously promised sacrifices to the Deity when he acquires wealth or has some desire fulfilled or when he has recovered from some illness or disease; putting on ornaments every day; not acting too freely with him; reciting his name and the name of his family in her songs; placing his hand on her loins, bosom, and forehead, and falling asleep after feeling the pleasure of his touch; sitting on his lap and falling asleep there; wishing to have a child by him; desiring not to live longer than he does; abstaining from revealing his secrets to others; dissuading him from vows and fasts by saying "let the sin fall upon me"; keeping vows and fasts along with him when it is impossible to change his mind on the subject; telling him that vows and fasts are difficult to be observed, even by herself, when she has any dispute with him about them; looking on her own wealth and his without any distinction; abstaining from going to public assemblies without him, and accompanying him when he desires her to do so; taking delight in using things previously used by him, and in eating food that he has left uneaten; venerating his family, his disposition, his skill in the arts, his learning, his caste, his complexion, his native country, his friends, his good qualities, his age, and his sweet temper; asking him to sing, and to do other suchlike things, if able to do them; going to him without paying any regard to fear, to cold, to heat, or to rain; saying with regard to the next world that he should be her lover even there; adapting her tastes, disposition, and actions to his liking; abstaining from sorcery; disputing continually with her mother on the subject of going to him, and when forcibly taken by her mother to some other place, expressing her desire to die by taking poison, by starving herself to death, by stabbing herself with some weapon, or by hanging herself; and, lastly, practice assuring the man of her constancy and love by means of her agents, and receiving money herself, but abstaining from any dispute with her mother with regard to pecuniary matters.

When the man sets out on a journey, she should make him swear that he will return quickly, and in his absence should put aside her vows of worshiping the Deity, and should wear no ornaments except those that are lucky. If the time fixed for his return has passed, she should endeavor to ascertain the real time of his return from omens, from the reports of the people, and from the position of the planets, the moon, and the stars. On occasions of amusement and of auspicious dreams she should wear no ornaments except those that are lucky. If, moreover, she feels melancholy, or sees any inauspicious omen, she should perform some rite to appease the Deity.

When the man does return home she should worship the god Kama (that is, the Indian Cupid), and offer oblations to other deities, and having caused a pot filled with water to be brought by her friends, she should perform the worship in honor of the crow who eats the offerings which we make to the manes of deceased relations. After the first visit is over, she should ask her lover also to perform certain rites, and this he will do if he is sufficiently attached to her.

Now, a man is said to be sufficiently attached to a woman when his love is disinterested; when he has the same object in view as his beloved one; when he is quite free from any suspicions on her account; and when he is indifferent to money with regard to her.

Such is the manner of a courtesan living with a man like a wife, and it is set forth here for the sake of guidance from the rules of Dattaka. What is not laid down here should be practiced according to the custom of the people and the nature of each individual man.

There are also two verses on the subject, as follows:

"The extent of the love of women is not known, even to those who are the objects of their affection, on account of its subtlety, and on account of the avarice, and natural intelligence of womankind."

"Women are hardly ever known in their true light, though they may love men, or become indifferent toward them; may give them delight, or abandon them; or may extract from them all the wealth that they may possess."

## Chapter III

*On the Means of Getting Money. On the Signs of Change of a Lover's Feelings, and on the Way to Get Rid of Him.*

Money is got out of a lover in two ways:

By natural or lawful means, and by artifices. Old authors are of the opinion that when a courtesan can get as much money as she wants from her lover, she should not make use of artifice. But Vatsyayana lays down that though she may get some money from him by natural means, yet when she makes use of artifice he gives her doubly more, and therefore artifice should be resorted to for the purpose of extorting money from him at all events.

Now, the artifices to be used for getting money from the lover are as follows:

1. Taking money from him on different occasions, for the purpose of purchasing various articles such as ornaments, food, drink, flowers, perfumes, and clothes, and either not buying them or getting from him more than their cost.

2. Praising his intelligence to his face.

3. Pretending to be obliged to make gifts on occasions of festivals connected with vows, trees, gardens, temples, or tanks.

4. Pretending that at the time of going to his house, her jewels have been stolen either by the king's guards or by robbers.

5. Alleging that her property has been destroyed by fire, by the falling of her house, or by the carelessness of the servants.

6. Pretending to have lost the ornaments of her lover along with her own.

7. Causing him to hear through other people of the expenses incurred by her in coming to see him.

8. Contracting debts for the sake of her lover.

9. Disputing with her mother on account of some expense, incurred by her for the lover, which was not approved of by her mother.

10. Not going to parties and festivities in the houses of her friends for the want of presents to make to them, she having previously informed her lover of the valuable presents given to her by these very friends.

11. Not performing certain festive rites under the pretense that she has no money to perform them with.

12. Engaging artists to do something for her lover.

13. Entertaining physicians and ministers for the purpose of attaining some object.

14. Assisting friends and benefactors both on festive occasions and in misfortune.

15. Performing household rites.

16. Having to pay the expenses of the ceremony of marriage of the son of a female friend.

17. Having to satisfy curious wishes during her state of pregnancy.

18. Pretending to be ill, and charging her cost of treatment.

19. Having to remove the troubles of a friend.

20. Selling some of her ornaments, so as to give her lover a present.

21. Pretending to sell some of her ornaments, furniture, or cooking utensils to a trader, who has already been tutored how to behave in the matter.

22. Having to buy cooking utensils of greater value than those of other people, so that they might be more easily dis-

tinguished, and not changed for others of an inferior description.

23. Remembering the former favors of her lover, and causing them always to be spoken of by her friends and followers.

24. Informing her lover of the great gains of other courtesans.

25. Describing before them, and in the presence of her lover, her own great gains, and making them out to be greater even than theirs, though such may not have been really the case.

26. Openly opposing her mother when she endeavors to persuade her to take up with men with whom she had been formerly acquainted, on account of the great gains to be got from them.

27. Lastly, pointing out to her lover the liberality of his rivals.

Thus ends discourse of the ways and means of getting money.

A woman should always know the state of the mind, of the feelings, and of the disposition of her lover toward her, from the changes of his temper, his manner, and the color of his face.

The behavior of a waning lover is as follows:

1. He gives the woman either less than is wanted or something other than that which is asked for.

2. He keeps her in hopes by promises.

3. He pretends to do one thing, and does something else.

4. He does not fulfill her desires.

5. He forgets his promises, or does something other than that which he has promised.

6. He speaks with his own servants in a mysterious way.

7. He sleeps in some other house under the pretense of having to do something for a friend.

8. Lastly, he speaks in private with the attendants of a woman with whom he was formerly acquainted.

Now, when a courtesan finds that her lover's disposition toward her is changing, she should get possession of all his best things before he becomes aware of her intentions, and allow a supposed creditor to take them away forcibly from her in satisfaction of some pretended debt. After this, if the lover is rich, and has always behaved well toward her, she should ever treat him with respect; but if he is poor and destitute she should get rid of him as if she had never been acquainted with him in any way before.

The means of getting rid of a lover are as follows:

1. Describing the habits and vices of the lover as disagreeable and censurable, with a sneer of the lip and a stamp of the foot.

2. Speaking on a subject with which he is not acquainted.

3. Showing no admiration for his learning, and passing a censure upon it.

4. Putting down his pride.

5. Seeking the company of men who are superior to him in learning and wisdom.

6. Showing a disregard for him on all occasions.

7. Censuring men possessed of the same faults as her lover.

8. Expressing dissatisfaction at the ways and means of enjoyment used by him.

9. Not giving him her mouth to kiss.

10. Refusing access to her jaghana, that is, the part of the body between the navel and the thighs.

11. Showing a dislike for the wounds made by his nails and teeth.

12. Not pressing close up against him at the time when he embraces her.

13. Keeping her limbs without movement at the time of congress.

14. Desiring him to enjoy her when he is fatigued.

15. Laughing at his attachment to her.

16. Not responding to his embraces.

17. Turning away from him when he begins to embrace her.

18. Pretending to be sleepy.

19. Going out visiting, or into company, when she perceives his desire to enjoy her during the daytime.

20. Misconstruing his words.

21. Laughing without any joke; or, at the time of any joke made by him, laughing under some other pretense.

22. Looking with side glances at her own attendants, and clapping her hands when he says anything.

23. Interrupting him in the middle of his stories, and beginning to tell other stories herself.

24. Reciting his faults and his vices, and declaring them to be incurable.

25. Saying words to her female attendants calculated to cut the heart of her lover to the quick.

26. Taking care not to look at him when he comes to her.

27. Asking from him what cannot be granted.

28. And, after all, finally dismissing him.

There are also two verses on this subject, as follows:

"The duty of a courtesan consists in forming connections with suitable men after due and full consideration, and attaching the person with whom she is united to herself; in obtaining wealth from the person who is attached to her; and then dismissing him after she has taken away all his possessions."

"A courtesan leading in this manner the life of a wife is not troubled with too many lovers, and yet obtains abundance of wealth."

## Chapter IV

### On Reunion with a Former Lover

When a courtesan abandons her present lover after all his wealth is exhausted, she may then consider about her reunion with a former lover. But she should return to him only if he has acquired fresh wealth, or is still wealthy, and if he is still attached to her. And if this man be living at the time with some other woman, she should consider well before she acts.

Now, such a man can be in only one of the six following conditions:

1. He may have left the first woman of his own accord, and may even have left another woman since then.
2. He may have been driven away from both women.
3. He may have left the one woman of his own accord, and been driven away by the other.
4. He may have left the one woman of his own accord and be living with another woman.
5. He may have been driven away from the one woman, and left the other of his own accord.
6. He may have been driven away by the one woman, and may be living with another.

(1). Now, if the man has left both women of his own accord, he should not be resorted to, because of the fickleness of his mind and his indifference to the excellences of both of them.

(2). As regards the man who may have been driven away from both women, if he has been driven away from the last one because the woman could get more money from some other man, then he should be resorted to, for if attached to the first woman he would give her more money through vanity and emulation to spite the other woman. But if he has been driven away by the woman on account of his poverty, or stinginess, he should not then be resorted to.

(3). In the case of the man who may have left the one woman of his own accord, and been driven away by the other, if he agrees to return to the former and give her plenty of money beforehand, then he should be resorted to.

(4). In the case of the man who may have left the one woman of his own accord, and be living with another woman, the former (wishing to take up with him again) should first ascertain if he left her in the first instance in the hope of finding some particular excellence in the other woman, and that not having found any such excellence, he was willing to come back to her, and to give her much money because of his conduct and because of his affection still existing for her.

Or whether, having discovered many faults in the other woman, he would now see even more excellences in herself than actually exist, and would be prepared to give her much money for these qualities.

Or, lastly, to consider whether he was a weak man, or a man fond of enjoying many women, or one who liked a poor woman, or one who never did anything for the woman that he was with. After maturely considering all these things, she should resort to him or not, according to circumstances.

(5). As regards the man who may have been driven away from the one woman, and left the other of his own accord, the former woman (wishing to reunite with him) should first ascertain whether he still has any affection for her, and would consequently spend much money upon her; or whether, being attached to her excellent qualities, he did not take delight in any other women; or whether, being driven away from her formerly before completely satisfying his sexual desires, he wished to get back to her so as to be revenged for the injury done to him; or whether he wished to create confidence in her mind, and then take back from her the wealth which she formerly took from him, and finally destroy her; or, lastly, whether he wished first to separate her from her present lover, and then to break away from her himself. If, after considering all these things, she is of opinion that his intentions are really pure and honest, she can reunite herself with him. But if his mind be at all tainted with evil intentions, he should be avoided.

(6). In the case of the man who may have been driven away by one woman, and be living with another, if the man makes overtures to return to the first one, the courtesan should consider well before she acts, and while the other woman is engaged in attracting him to herself, she should try in her turn (though keeping herself behind the scenes) to gain him over, on the grounds of any of the following considerations:

1. That he was driven away unjustly and for no proper reason, and now that he has gone to another woman, every effort must be used to bring him back to myself.

2. That if he were once to consort with me again, he would break away from the other woman.

3. That the pride of my present lover would be put down by means of the former one.

4. That he has become wealthy, has secured a higher position, and holds a place of authority under the king.

5. That he is separate from his wife.

6. That he is now independent.

7. That he lives apart from his father or brother.

8. That by making peace with him, I shall be able to get hold of a very rich man, who is now prevented from coming to me by my present lover.

9. That as he is not respected by his wife, I shall now be able to separate him from her.

10. That the friend of this man loves my rival, who hates me cordially. I shall therefore by this means separate the friend from his mistress.

11. And, lastly, I shall bring discredit upon him by bringing him back to me, thus showing the fickleness of his mind.

When a courtesan is resolved to take up again with a former lover, her Pithamarda and other servants should tell him that his former expulsion from the woman's house was caused by the wickedness of her mother; that the woman loved him just as much as ever at that time, but could not help the occurrence because of her deference to her mother's will; that she hated the union of her present lover, and disliked him excessively. In addition to this, they should create confidence in his mind by speaking to him of her former love for him, and should allude to the mark of that love that she has ever remembered. This mark of her love should be connected with some kind of pleasure that may have been practiced by him, such as his way of kissing her, or manner of having connection with her.

Thus ends discourse of the ways of bringing about a reunion with a former lover.

When a woman has to choose between two lovers, one of whom was formerly united with her, while the other is a stranger, the Acharyas (sages) are of the opinion that the first one is preferable because, his disposition and character being already known by previous careful observation, he can be easily pleased and satisfied; but Vatsyayana thinks that a former lover, having already spent a great deal of his wealth, is not able or willing to give much money again, and is not therefore to be relied upon so much as a stranger. Particular cases differing from this general rule may, however, arise because of the different natures of men.

There are also verses on these subjects, as follows:

"Reunion with a former lover may be desirable so as to

separate some particular woman from some particular man, or some particular man from some particular woman, or to have a certain effect upon the present lover."

"When a man is excessively attached to a woman, he is afraid of her coming into contact with other men; he does not then regard or notice her faults; and he gives her much wealth through fear of her leaving him."

"A courtesan should be agreeable to the man who is attached to her, and despise the man who does not care for her. If while she is living with one man, a messenger comes to her from some other man, she may either refuse to listen to any negotiations on his part, or appoint a fixed time for him to visit her, but she should not leave the man who may be living with her and who may be attached to her."

"A wise woman should renew her connection with a former lover only if she is satisfied that good fortune, gain, love, and friendship are likely to be the result of such a reunion."

## Chapter v

### On Different Kinds of Gain

When a courtesan is able to realize much money every day, by reason of many customers, she should not confine herself to a single lover; under such circumstances she should fix`her rate for one night, after considering the place, the season, and the condition of the people, also having regard to her own good qualities and good looks, and after comparing her rates with those of other courtesans. She can inform her lovers and friends and acquaintances about these charges. If, however, she can obtain great gain from a single lover, she may resort to him alone, and live with him like a wife.

Now, the sages are of the opinion that when a courtesan has the chance of equal gain from two lovers at the same time, a preference should be given to the one who would give her the kind of thing she wants. But Vatsyayana says that the preference should be given to the one who gives her gold, because it cannot be taken back like some other things, it can be easily received, and it is also the means of procuring anything that may be wished for. Of such things as gold, silver, copper, bell metal, iron, pots, furniture, beds, upper garments, undervestments, fragrant substances, vessels made of gourds, ghee, oil, corn, cattle, and other things of like nature, the first, namely, gold, is superior to all the others.

When the same labor is required to gain any two lovers or when the same kind of thing is to be got from each of them, the choice should be made by the advice of a friend, or

226

it may be made from the lovers' personal qualities, or from the signs of good or bad fortune that may be connected with them.

When there are two lovers, one of whom is attached to the courtesan, and the other is simply very generous, the sages say that a preference should be given to the generous lover; but Vatsyayana is of the opinion that the one who is really attached to the courtesan should be preferred, because he can be made to be generous, even as a miser gives money if he becomes fond of a woman, but a man who is simply generous cannot be made to love with real attachment. But among those who are attached to her, if there is one who is poor, and one who is rich, the preference is of course to be given to the latter.

When there are two lovers, one of whom is generous, and the other ready to do any service for the courtesan, some sages say that the one who is ready to do the service should be preferred; but Vatsyayana is of the opinion that a man who does a service thinks that he has gained his object when he has done something once, but a generous man does not care for what he has given before. Even here the choice should be guided by the likelihood of the future good to be derived from her union with either of them.

When one of two lovers is grateful, and the other liberal, some sages say that the liberal one should be preferred; but Vatsyayana is of the opinion that the former should be chosen, because liberal men are generally haughty, plain-spoken, and wanting in consideration toward others. Even though these liberal men have been on friendly terms for a long time, yet if they see any fault in the courtesan, or are told lies about her by some other woman, they do not care for past services, but leave abruptly. On the other hand, the grateful man does not at once break off from her, because of a regard for the pains she may have taken to please him. In this case also, the choice is to be guided with regard to what may happen in the future.

When an occasion for complying with the request of a friend, and a chance of getting money come together, the sages say that the chance of getting money should be preferred. But Vatsyayana thinks that money can be obtained tomorrow as well as today, but if the request of a friend be not at once complied with, he may become disaffected. Even here, in making the choice, regard must be paid to future good fortune.

On such an occasion, however, the courtesan might pacify her friend by pretending to have some work to do, and telling him that his request will be complied with next day, and in this way secure the chance of getting the money that has been offered her.

When the chance of getting money, and the chance of avoiding some disaster come at the same time, the sages are of the opinion that the chance of getting money should be preferred, but Vatsyayana says that money has only a limited importance, while a disaster that is once averted may never occur again. Here, however, the choice should be guided by the greatness or smallness of the disaster.

The gains of the wealthiest and best kind of courtesans are to be spent as follows:

Building temples, tanks, and gardens; giving a thousand cows to different Brahmans; carrying on the worship of the gods, and celebrating festivals in their honor; and, lastly, performing such vows as may be within their means.

The gains of other courtesans are to be spent as follows:

Having a white dress to wear every day; getting sufficient food and drink to satisfy hunger and thirst; eating daily a perfumed tambula, that is, a mixture of betel nut and betel leaves; and wearing ornaments gilt with gold. The sages say that these represent the gains of all the middle and lower classes of courtesans, but Vatsyayana is of the opinion that their gains cannot be calculated, or fixed in any way, as these depend on the influences of the place, the customs of the people, their own appearance, and many other things.

When a courtesan wants to keep some particular man

from some other woman, or wishes to get him away from some woman to whom he may be attached, or to deprive some woman of the gains realized by her from him; or if she thinks that she would raise her position, or enjoy some great good fortune, or become desirable to all men by uniting herself with this man; or if she wishes to get his assistance in averting some misfortune, or is really attached to him and loves him, or wishes to injure somebody through this means, or has regard to some former favor conferred upon her by him, or wishes to be united with him merely from desire—for any of the above reasons she should agree to take from him only a small sum of money in a friendly way.

When a courtesan intends to abandon a particular lover and take up with another one; or when she has reason to believe that her lover will shortly leave her, and return to his wives; or that having squandered all his money, and become penniless, his guardian or master or father would come and take him away; or that her lover is about to lose his position; or, lastly, that he is of a very fickle mind; she should, under any of these circumstances, endeavor to get as much money as she can from him as soon as possible.

On the other hand, when the courtesan thinks that her lover is about to receive valuable presents, or get a place of authority from the king, or be near the time of inheriting a fortune, or that his ship will soon arrive laden with merchandise, or that he has large stocks of corn and other commodities, or that if anything was done for him it would not be done in vain, or that he is always true to his word, then should she have regard to her future welfare, and live with the man like a wife.

There are also verses on these subjects, as follows:

"In considering her present gains, and her future welfare, a courtesan should avoid such persons as have gained their means of subsistence with very great difficulty, as well as those who have become selfish and hardhearted by becoming the favorites of kings."

"She should make every endeavor to unite herself with prosperous and well-to-do people and with those whom it is dangerous to avoid or to slight in any way. Even at some cost to herself she should become acquainted with energetic and liberal-minded men, who when pleased would give her a large sum of money, even for very little service, or for some small thing."

## Chapter VI

### On Gains and Losses; Attendant Gains, Losses, and Doubts. And, Lastly, on the Different Kinds of Courtesans

It sometimes happens that while gains are being sought for, or expected to be realized, only losses are the result of our efforts. The causes of these losses are:

> Weakness of intellect
> Excessive love
> Excessive pride
> Excessive self-conceit
> Excessive simplicity
> Excessive confidence
> Excessive anger
> Carelesness
> Recklesness
> Influence of evil genius
> Accidental circumstances

The results of these losses are:

> Expense incurred without any result
> Destruction of future good fortune
> Stoppage of gains about to be realized
> Loss of what is already obtained
> Acquisition of a sour temper
> Becoming unamiable to everybody
> Injury to head
> Loss of hair, and other accidents

Now, gain is of three kinds: gain of wealth, gain of religious merit, and gain of pleasure; and similarly, loss is of three kinds: loss of wealth, loss of religious merit, and loss of pleasure. At the time when gains are sought for, if other gains come along with them, these are called attendant gains. When gain is uncertain, the doubt of its being a gain is called a simple doubt. When there is a doubt whether either of two things will happen or not, it is called a mixed doubt. If while one thing is being done, two results take place, it is called a combination of two results; and if several results follow from the same action, it is called a combination of results on every side.

We shall now give examples of the above.

As already stated, gain is of three kinds; and loss, which is opposed to gain, is also of three kinds.

(*a*). When by living with a great man a courtesan acquires present wealth, and in addition to this becomes acquainted with other people, and thus obtains a chance of future fortune and an accession of wealth, and becomes desirable to all, this is called a gain of wealth attended by other gain.

(*b*). When by living with a man a courtesan simply gets money, this is called a gain of wealth not attended by any other gain.

(*c*). When a courtesan receives money from other people besides her lover, the results are: the chance of the loss of future good from her present lover; the chance of disaffection of a man securely attached to her; the hatred of all; and the chance of a union with some low person tending to destroy her future good. This gain is called a gain of wealth attended by losses.

(*d*). When a courtesan at her own expense, and without any results in the shape of gain, has connection with a great man, or with an avaricious minister, for the sake of diverting some misfortune or removing some cause that may be threatening the destruction of a great gain, this loss is said to be a loss of wealth attended by gains of the future good which it may bring about.

(*e*). When a courtesan is kind, even at her own expense, to a man who is very stingy, or to a man proud of his looks, or to an ungrateful man skilled in gaining the heart of others, without any good resulting from these connections to her in the end, this loss is called a loss of wealth not attended by any gain.

(*f*). When a courtesan is kind to any such men as described above, but who in addition are favorites of the king, and who, moreover, are cruel and powerful, without any good result in the end, and with a chance of her being turned away at any moment, this loss is called a loss of wealth attended by other losses.

In this way gains and losses, and attendant gains and losses in religious merit and in pleasures, may become known to the reader, and combinations of all of them may also be made.

Thus end the remarks on gains and losses, and attendant gains and losses.

In the next place we come to doubts, which are again of three kinds: doubts about wealth, doubts about religious merit, and doubts about pleasures.

The following are examples.

(*a*). When a courtesan is not certain how much a man may give her or spend upon her, this is called a doubt about wealth.

(*b*). When a courtesan feels doubtful whether she is right in entirely abandoning a lover from whom she is unable to get money, she having taken all his wealth from him in the first instance, this doubt is called a doubt about religious merit.

(*c*). When a courtesan is unable to get hold of a lover to her liking, and is uncertain whether she will derive any pleasure from a person surrounded by his family, or from a low person, this is called a doubt about pleasure.

(*d*). When a courtesan is uncertain whether some power-ful but low-principled fellow would cause loss to her because of her being civil to him, this is called a doubt about the loss of wealth.

(*e*). When a courtesan feels doubtful whether she would lose religious merit by abandoning a man who is attached to her without giving him the slightest favor, and thereby causing him unhappiness in this world and the next,[1] this doubt is called a doubt about the loss of religious merit.

(*f*). When a courtesan is uncertain as to whether she might create disaffection by speaking out, and revealing her love, and thus not get her desire satisfied, this is called a doubt about the loss of pleasure.

Thus end the remarks on doubts.

## Mixed Doubts

(*a*). The intercourse or connection with a stranger whose disposition is unknown, and who may have been introduced by a lover or by one who possessed authority, may be productive either of gain or loss, and therefore this is called a mixed doubt about the gain and loss of wealth.

(*b*). When a courtesan is requested by a friend, or is im-pelled by pity to have intercourse with a learned Brahman, a religious student, a sacrificer, a devotee, or an ascetic who may have all fallen in love with her, and who may be consequently at the point of death, by doing this she might either gain or lose religious merit, and therefore this is called a mixed doubt about the gain or loss of religious merit.

(*c*). If a courtesan relies solely upon the report of other people (hearsay) about a man, and goes to him without ascer-taining herself whether he possesses good qualities or not, she may either gain or lose pleasure in proportion as he may be

---

[1] The souls of men who die with their desires unfulfilled are said to go to the world of the manes, and not direct to the Supreme Spirit.

good or bad, and therefore this is called a mixed doubt about the gain and loss of pleasure.

Uddalika has described the gains and losses on both sides as follows:

(*a*). If, when living with a lover, a courtesan gets both wealth and pleasure from him, it is called a gain on both sides.

(*b*). When a courtesan lives with a lover at her own expense without getting any profit out of it, and the lover even takes back from her what he may have formerly given her, it is called a loss on both sides.

(*c*). When a courtesan is uncertain whether a new acquaintance would become attached to her, and, moreover, if he became attached to her, whether he would give her anything, it is called a doubt on both sides about gains.

(*d*). When a courtesan is uncertain whether a former enemy, if made up to by her at her own expense, would do her some injury because of his grudge against her; or, if becoming attached to her, would angrily take away from her anything that he may have given to her, this is called a doubt on both sides about loss.

Babhravya has described the gains and losses on both sides as follows:

(*a*). When a courtesan can get money from a man whom she may go to see, and also money from a man whom she may not go to see, this is called a gain on both sides.

(*b*). When a courtesan has to incur further expense if she goes to see a man, and yet runs the risk of incurring an irremediable loss if she does not go to see him, this is called a loss on both sides.

(*c*). When a courtesan is uncertain whether a particular man would give her anything on her going to see him, without incurring expense on her part, or whether on her neglecting him another man would give her something, this is called a doubt on both sides about gain.

(*d*). When a courtesan is uncertain whether, on going at her own expense to see an old enemy, he would take back from her what he may have given her, or whether by her not going to see him he would cause some disaster to fall upon her, this is called a doubt on both sides about loss.

By combining the above, the following six kinds of mixed results are produced:

(*a*). Gain on one side, and loss on the other.

(*b*). Gain on one side, and doubt of gain on the other.

(*c*). Gain on one side, and doubt of loss on the other.

(*d*). Loss on one side, and doubt of gain on the other.

(*e*). Doubt of gain on one side, and doubt of loss on the other.

(*e*). Doubt of gain on one side, and doubt of loss on the other.

(*f*). Doubt of loss on one side, and loss on the other.

A courtesan, having considered all the above things and taken counsel with her friends, should act so as to acquire gain, the chances of great gain, and the warding off of any great disaster. Religious merit and pleasure should also be formed into separate combination like those of wealth, and then all should be combined with each other, so as to form new combinations.

When a courtesan consorts with men, she should cause each of them to give her money as well as pleasure. At particular times, such as the Spring Festivals, and so on, she should make her mother announce to the various men that on a certain day her daughter would remain with the man who would gratify such and such a desire of hers.

When young men approach her with delight, she should think of what she may accomplish through them.

The combination of gains and losses on all sides are: gain on one side, and loss on all others; loss on one side, and gain on all others; gain on all sides, loss on all sides.

A courtesan should also consider doubts about gain and doubts about loss with reference both to wealth, religious merit, and pleasure.

Thus ends the consideration of gain, loss, attendant gains, attendant losses, and doubts.

The different kinds of courtesans are:

> A bawd
> A female attendant
> An unchaste woman
> A dancing girl
> A female artisan
> A woman who has left her family
> A woman living on her beauty
> And, finally, a regular courtesan

All the above kinds of courtesans are acquainted with various kinds of men, and should consider the ways of getting money from them, of pleasing them, of separating themselves from them, and of reuniting with them. They should also take into consideration particular gains and losses, attendant gains and losses, and doubts in accordance with their several conditions.

Thus ends the consideration of courtesans.

There are also two verses on the subject, as follows:

"Men want pleasure, while women want money, and therefore this Part, which treats of the means of gaining wealth, should be studied."

"There are some women who seek for love, and there are others who seek for money; for the former the ways of love are told in previous portions of this work, while the ways of getting money, as practiced by courtesans, are described in this Part."

# PART SEVEN

*On the Means of Attracting Others to Yourself*

## Chapter 1

### On Personal Adornment; On Subjugating the Hearts of Others; and on Tonic Medicines

When a person fails to obtain the object of his desires by any of the ways previously related, he should then have recourse to other ways of attracting others to himself.

Now, good looks, qualities, youth, and liberality are the chief and most natural means of making a person agreeable in the eyes of others. But in the absence of these, a man or woman must have resort to artificial means, or to art, and the following are some recipes that may be found useful:

(*a*). An ointment made of the *Tabernaemontana coronaria*, the *Costus speciosus* or arabicus, and the *Flacourtia Cataphracta*, can be used as an unguent of adornment.

(*b*). If a fine powder is made of the above plants, and applied to the wick of a lamp, which is made to burn with the oil of blue vitriol, the black pigment or lampblack produced therefrom, when applied to the eyelashes, has the effect of making a person look lovely.

(*c*). The oil of the hogweed, the *Echites putescens*, the sarina plant, the yellow amaranth, and the leaf of the nymphæ, if applied to the body, has the same effect.

(*d*). A black pigment from the same plants produces a similar effect.

(*e*). By eating the powder of the *Nelumbium speciosum*, the blue lotus, and the *Mesna roxburghii,* with ghee and honey, a man becomes lovely in the eyes of others.

(*f*). The above things, together with the *Tabernaemontana coronaria,* and the *Xanthochymus pictorius,* if used as an ointment, produce the same results.

(*g*). If the bone of a peacock or of a hyena be covered with gold, and tied on the right hand, it makes a man lovely in the eyes of other people.

(*h*). In the same way, if a bead, made of the seed of the jujube, or of the conch shell, be enchanted by the incantations mentioned in the Arthava Veda, or by the incantations of those well skilled in the science of magic, and tied on the hand, it produces the same result as described above.

(*i*). When a female attendant arrives at the age of puberty, her master should keep her secluded, and when men ardently desire her because of her seclusion, and because of the difficulty of approaching her, he should then bestow her hand on such a person as may endow her with wealth and happiness.

This is a means of increasing the loveliness of a person in the eyes of others.

In the same way, when the daughter of a courtesan arrives at the age of puberty, the mother should get together a lot of young men of the same age, disposition, and knowledge as her daughter, and tell them that she would give her in marriage to the person who would give her presents of a particular kind.

After this, the daughter should be kept in seclusion as far as possible, and the mother should give her in marriage to the man who may be ready to give her the presents agreed upon. If the mother is unable to get so much out of the man, she should show some of her own things as having been given to the daughter by the bridegroom.

Or the mother may allow her daughter to be married to the man privately, as if she were ignorant of the whole affair, and then, pretending that it has come to her knowledge, she may give her consent to the union.

The daughter, too, should make herself attractive to the sons of wealthy citizens, unknown to her mother, and make them attached to her, and for this purpose should meet them at the time of learning to sing, and in places where music is played, and at the houses of other people, and then request her mother, through a female friend or servant, to be allowed to unite herself to the man who is most agreeable to her.[1]

When the daughter of a courtesan is thus given to a man, the ties of marriage should be observed for one year, and after that she may do what she likes. But even after the end of the year, when otherwise engaged, if she should be now and then invited by her first husband to come and see him, she should put aside her present gain, and go to him for the night.

Such is the mode of temporary marriage among courtesans, and of increasing their loveliness and their value in the eyes of others. What has been said about them should also be understood to apply to the daughters of dancing women, whose mothers should give them only to such persons as are likely to become useful to them in various ways.

Thus ends discourse of the ways of making oneself lovely in the eyes of others.

(*a*). If a man, after anointing his lingam with a mixture of the powders of the white thorn apple, the long pepper and the black pepper, and honey, engages in sexual union with a woman, he makes her subject to his will.

(*b*). The application of a mixture of the leaf of the plant vatodbhranta, of the flowers thrown on a human corpse when carried out to be burned, and of the powder of the bones of the peacock, and of the jiwanjiva bird produces the same effect.

[1] It is a custom of the courtesans of Oriental countries to give their daughters temporarily in marriage when they come of age, and after they have received an education in the *Kama Sutra* and other arts.

(*c*). The remains of a kite who has died a natural death, ground into powder, and mixed with cowhage and honey, has also the same effect.

(*d*). Anointing oneself with an ointment made of the plant *Emblica myrobolans* has the power of subjecting women to one's will.

(*e*). If a man cuts into small pieces the sprouts of the vajnasunhi plant, and dips them into a mixture of red arsenic and sulphur, and then dries them seven times, and applies this powder mixed with honey to his lingam, he can subjugate a woman to his will directly he has had sexual union with her; or if by burning these very sprouts at night and looking at the smoke, he sees a golden moon behind, he will then be successful with any woman; or if he throws some of the powder of these same sprouts mixed with the excrement of a monkey upon a maiden, she will not be given in marriage to anybody else.

(*f*). If pieces of the orrisroot are dressed with the oil of the mango, and placed for six months in a hole made in the trunk of the sisu tree, and are then taken out and made up into an ointment, and applied to the lingam, this is said to serve as the means of subjugating women.

(*g*). If the bone of a camel is dipped into the juice of the plant *Eclipta prostata,* and then burned, and the black pigment produced from its ashes is placed in a box also made of the bone of a camel, and applied together with antimony to the eyelashes with a pencil also made of the bone of a camel, then that pigment is said to be very pure, and wholesome for the eyes, and serves as a means of subjugating others to the person who uses it. The same effect can be produced by black pigment made of the bones of hawks, vultures, and peacocks.

Thus ends discourse of the ways of subjugating others to one's own will.

Now, the means of increasing sexual vigor are as follows:

(*a*). A man obtains sexual vigor by drinking milk mixed with sugar, the root of the uchchata plant, the pipar chaba, and licorice.

(*b*). Drinking milk mixed with sugar, and having the testicle of a ram or a goat boiled in it, is also productive of vigor.

(*c*). The drinking of the juice of the *Hedysarum gangeticum*, the kuili, and the kshirika plant, mixed with milk, produces the same effect.

(*d*). The seed of long pepper, along with the seeds of the *Sansevieria roxburghiana*, and the *Hedysarum gangeticum* plant, all pounded together, and mixed with milk, is productive of a similar result.

(*e*). According to ancient authors, if a man pounds the seeds or roots of the *Trapa bispinosa*, the kasurika, the tuscan jasmine, and licorice, together with the kshirikapoli (a kind of onion), and puts the powder into milk mixed with sugar and ghee, and having boiled the whole mixture on a moderate fire, drinks the paste so formed, he will be able to enjoy innumerable women.

(*f*). In the same way, if a man mixes rice with the eggs of the sparrow, and having boiled this in milk, adds to it ghee and honey, and drinks as much of it as is necessary, this will produce the same effect.

(*g*). If a man takes the outer covering of sesame seeds, and soaks them with the eggs of sparrows, and then, having boiled them in milk, mixed with sugar and ghee, along with the fruits of the *Trapa bispinosa* and the kasurika plant, and adds to it the flour of wheat and beans, and then drinks this composition, he is said to be able to enjoy many women.

(*h*). If ghee, honey, sugar, and licorice in equal quantities, the juice of the fennel plant, and milk are mixed together, this nectar-like composition is said to be holy, and provocative of sexual vigor, a preservative of life, and sweet to the taste.

(*i*). The drinking of a paste composed of the *Asparagus*

*racemosus,* the shvadaushtra plant, the guduchi plant, the long pepper, and licorice, boiled in milk, honey, and ghee, in the spring, is said to have the same effect as the above.

(*j*). Boiling the *Asparagus racemosus* and the shvadaushtra plant, along with the pounded fruits of the *Premna spinosa* in water, and drinking the same, is said to act in the same way.

(*k*). Drinking boiled ghee, or clarified butter, in the morning, during the spring season, is said to be beneficial to health and strength, and agreeable to the taste.

(*l*). If the powder of the seed of the shvadaushtra plant and the flour of barley are mixed together in equal parts, and a portion of it, two palas in weight, is eaten every morning on getting up, it has the same effect as the preceding recipe.

There are also verses on the subject, as follows:

"The means [2] of producing love and sexual vigor should be learned from the science of medicine, from the Vedas, from those who are learned in the arts of magic, and from confidential relatives. No means should be tried which are doubtful in their effects, which are likely to cause injury to the body, which involve the death of animals, or which bring us in contact with impure things. Only such means should be used as are holy, acknowledged to be good, and approved of by Brahmans and friends."

[2] From the earliest times Oriental authors have concerned themselves with aphrodisiacs. The following note on the subject is taken from page 29 of a translation of the Hindu *Art of Love,* otherwise the *Ananga Ranga:* "Most Eastern treatises divide aphrodisiacs into two different kinds: (1) the mechanical or natural, such as scarification, flagellation, etc.; and (2) the medicinal or artificial. To the former belong the application of insects, as is practiced by some savage races; and all Orientalists will remember the tale of the old Brahman whose young wife insisted upon his being again stung by a wasp."

## Chapter II

### On the Ways of Exciting Desire; and on Miscellaneous Experiments and Recipes

If a man is unable to satisfy a Hastini, or elephant woman, he should have recourse to various means to excite her passion. At the commencement he should rub her yoni with his hand or fingers, and not begin to have intercourse with her until she becomes excited, or experiences pleasure. This is one way of exciting a woman.

Or he may make use of certain Apadravyas, or things which are put on or around the lingam to supplement its length or its thickness, so as to fit it to the yoni. In the opinion of Babhravya, these Apadravyas should be made of gold, silver, copper, iron, ivory, buffalo's horn, various kinds of wood, tin, or lead, and should be soft, cool, provocative of sexual vigor, and well fitted to serve the intended purpose. Vatsyayana, however, says that they may be made according to the natural liking of each individual.

The following are the different kinds of Apadravyas:

1. "The armlet" (Valaya) should be of the same size as the lingam, and should have its outer surface made rough with globules.

2. "The couple" (Sanghati) is formed of two armlets.

3. "The bracelet" (Chudaka) is made by joining three or more armlets, until they come up to the required length of the lingam.

4. "The single bracelet" is formed by wrapping a single wire around the lingam, according to its dimensions.

5. The Kantuka or Jalaka is a tube open at both ends, with a hole through it, outwardly rough and studded with soft globules, and made to fit the size of the yoni, and tied to the waist.

When such a thing cannot be obtained, then a tube made of the wood apple, or tubular stalk of the bottle gourd, or a reed made soft with oil and extracts of plants, and tied to the waist with string, may be made use of, as well as a row of soft pieces of wood tied together.

The above are the things that can be used in connection with, or in the place of, the lingam.

The people of the southern countries think that true sexual pleasure cannot be obtained without perforating the lingam, and they therefore cause it to be pierced like the lobes of the ears of an infant pierced for earrings.

Now, when a young man perforates his lingam he should pierce it with a sharp instrument, and then stand in water as long as the blood continues to flow. At night he should engage in sexual intercourse, even with vigor, so as to clean the hole. After this he should continue to wash the hole with decoctions, and increase the size by putting into it small pieces of cane, and the *Wrightea antidysenterica,* thus gradually enlarging the orifice. It may also be washed with licorice mixed with honey, and the size of the hole increased by the fruit stalks of the simapatra plant. The hole should also be anointed with a small quantity of oil.

In the hole made in the lingam a man may put Apadravyas of various forms, such as the "round," the "round on one side," the "wooden mortar," the "flower," the "armlet," the "bone of the heron," the "goad of the elephant," the "collection of eight balls," the "lock of hair," the "place where four roads meet," and other things named according to their forms and means of using them. All these Apadravyas should be rough on the outside according to their requirements.

The ways of enlarging the lingam must now be related.

When a man wishes to enlarge his lingam, he should rub it with the bristles of certain insects that live in trees, and then, after rubbing it for ten nights with oils, he should again rub it with the bristles as before. By continuing to do this a swelling will be gradually produced in the lingam, and he should then lie on a cot, and cause his lingam to hang down through a hole in the cot. After this, he should take away all the pain from the swelling by using cool concoctions. The swelling, which is called "Suka," and is often brought about among the people of the Dravidian country, lasts for life.

If the lingam is rubbed with the following things, namely, the plant *Physalis flexuosa*, the shavara-kandaka plant, the jalasuka plant, the fruit of the eggplant, the butter of a she-buffalo, the hasti-charma plant, and the juice of the vajrarasna plant, a swelling lasting for one month will be produced.

By rubbing it with oil boiled in the concoctions of the above things, the same effect will be produced, but lasting for six months.

The enlargement of the lingam is also effected by rubbing it or moistening it with oil boiled on a moderate fire along with the seeds of the pomegranate, and the cucumber, the juices of the valuka plant, the hasti-charma plant, and the eggplant.

In addition to the above, other means may be learned from experience and confidential persons.

The miscellaneous experiments and recipes are as follows:

(*a*). If a man mixes the powder of the milk hedge plant and the kantaka plant with the excrement of a monkey and the powdered root of the lanjalika plant, and throws this mixture on a woman, she will not love anybody else afterward.

(*b*). If a man thickens the juice of the fruits of the *Cassia fistula* and the *Eugenia jambolana* by mixing them with the powder of the soma plant, the *Vernonia anthelmintica*, the *Eclipta prostata*, and the lohopa-jihirka, and applies this composition to the yoni of a woman, and then has sexual intercourse with her, his love for her will be destroyed.

(*c*). The same effect is produced if a man has connection with a woman who has bathed in the buttermilk of a she-buffalo mixed with the powders of gopalika plant, the banupadika plant, and the yellow amaranth.

(*d*). An ointment made of the flowers of the *Nauclea cadamba*, the hog plum, and the *Eugenia jambolana*, and used by a woman, causes her to be dislike by her husband.

(*e*). Garlands made of the above flowers, when worn by the woman, produce the same effect.

(*f*). An ointment made of the fruit of the *Asteracantha longifolia* (kokilaksha) will contract the yoni of a Hastini, or elephant woman, and this contraction lasts for one night.

(*g*). An ointment made by pounding the roots of the *Nelumbium speciosum* and of the blue lotus, and the powder of the plant *Physalis flexuosa* mixed with ghee and honey, will enlarge the yoni of the Mrigi, or deer woman.

(*h*). An ointment made of the fruit of the *Emblica myrobolans*, soaked in the milky juice of the milk hedge plant, of the soma plant, the *Calotropis gigantea*, and the juice of the fruit of the *Vernonia anthelmintica*, will make the hair white.

(*i*). The juice of the roots of the madayantika plant, the yellow amaranth, the anjanika plant, the *Clitoria ternatea*, and the shlakshnaparni plant, used as a lotion, will make the hair grow.

(*j*). An ointment made by boiling the above roots in oil, and rubbed in, will make the hair black, and will also gradually restore hair that has fallen off.

(*k*). If lac is saturated seven times in the sweat of the testicle of a white horse, and applied to a red lip, the lip will become white.

(*l*). The color of the lips can be regained by means of the madayantika and other plants mentioned above under (*i*).

(*m*). A woman who hears a man playing on a reed pipe which has been dressed with the juices of the bahupadika plant, the *Tabernaemontana coronaria*, the *Costus speciosus* or arabicus, the *Pinus deodora*, the *Euphorbia antiquorum*, the vajra and the kantaka plant, becomes his slave.

(*n*). If food be mixed with the fruit of the thorn apple (datura) it causes intoxication.

(*o*). If water be mixed with oil and the ashes of any kind of grass except the kusha grass, it becomes the color of milk.

(*p*). If yellow myrobolans, the hog plum, the shrawana plant, and the priyangu plant be all pounded together, and applied to iron pots, these pots become red.

(*q*). If a lamp, trimmed with oil extracted from the shrawana and priyangu plants (its wick being made of cloth and the slough of the skins of snakes), is lighted, and long pieces of wood placed near it, those pieces of wood will resemble so many snakes.

(*r*). Drinking the milk of a white cow who has a white calf at her foot is auspicious, produces fame, and preserves life.

(*s*). The blessings of venerable Brahmans, well propitiated, have the same effect.

There are also some verses in conclusion:

"Thus have I written in a few words these *Aphorisms on Love,* after reading the texts of ancient authors, and following the ways of enjoyment mentioned in them.

"He who is acquainted with the true principles of this science pays regard to Dharma, Artha, Kama, and to his own experiences, as well as to the teachings of others, and does not act simply on the dictates of his own desire. As for the errors in the science of love which I have mentioned in this work, on my own authority as an author, I have, immediately after mentioning them, carefully censured and prohibited them.

"An act is never looked upon with indulgence for the simple

reason that it is authorized by the science, because it ought to be remembered that it is the intention of the science that the rules which it contains should be acted upon only in particular cases. After reading and considering the works of Babhravya and other ancient authors, and thinking over the meaning of the rules given by them, the *Kama Sutra* was composed, according to the precepts of Holy Writ, for the benefit of the world, by Vatsyayana, while leading the life of a religious student, and wholly engaged in the contemplation of the Deity.

"This work is not intended to be used merely as an instrument for satisfying our desires. A person acquainted with the true principles of this science, and who preserves his Dharma, Artha, and Kama, and has regard for the practices of the people, is sure to obtain the mastery over his senses.

"In short, an intelligent and prudent person, attending to Dharma and Artha, and attending to Kama also, without becoming the slave of his passions, obtains success in everything that he may undertake."